"FOUL DEMONS, COME OUT!"

"FOUL DEMONS, COME OUT!"

The Rhetoric of
Twentieth-Century American Faith Healing

Stephen J. Pullum

PRAEGER

Westport, Connecticut
London

Library of Congress Cataloging-in-Publication Data

Pullum, Stephen Jackson, 1957–
   "Foul demons, come out!" : the rhetoric of twentieth-century
American faith healing / Stephen J. Pullum.
     p. cm.
   Includes bibliographical references and index.
   ISBN 0–275–96083–8 (alk. paper)
   1. Healers—United States—History—20th century. 2. Spiritual
healing—United States—History—20th century. 3. Rhetoric—
Religious aspects—Christianity—History—20th century.
   I. Title.
   BT732.55.P85   1999
   234'.131'09730904—dc21   98–47817

British Library Cataloguing in Publication Data is available.

Library of Congress Catalog Card Number: 98–47817
ISBN: 0–275–96083–8

First published in 1999

Praeger Publishers, 88 Post Road West, Westport, CT 06881
An imprint of Greenwood Publishing Group, Inc.
www.praeger.com

Printed in the United States of America

The paper used in this book complies with the
Permanent Paper Standard issued by the National
Information Standards Organization (Z39.48–1984).

10 9 8 7 6 5 4 3 2 1

Copyright Acknowledgments

The author and publisher gratefully acknowledge permission to use the following material:

Excerpts from Stephen J. Pullum, "His Speech Betrayeth Him: The Healing Rhetoric of Ernest Angley," *The Journal of Communication and Religion* 14.1 (September 1991). Reprinted with permission of the Religious Communication Association.

Excerpts from Stephen J. Pullum, "Sisters of the Spirit: The Rhetorical Methods of Female Faith Healers Aimee Semple McPherson, Kathryn Kuhlman, and Gloria Copeland," *The Journal of Communication and Religion* 16.2 (September 1993). Reprinted with the permission of the Religious Communication Association.

Excerpts in chapter 2 from audiotapes (nos. 1, 50A, 50B, 56, 63, 74, 118A, 118B, 246, and 410) and videotapes (nos. 1 and 2) in the William Branham Collection #123. Courtesy of the Billy Graham Center Archives, Wheaton College, Wheaton, Illinois. Used with permission of Pearry Green.

To Jennifer, Skyler, Maddison, and Lindsey

Contents

Contents

Acknowledgments

I am indebted to a number of people who helped make this book a reality. Ms. Janyce Nasgowitz, reference archivist, at the Billy Graham Center Archives at Wheaton College helped me locate invaluable information on William Branham and Kathryn Kuhlman. I am equally indebted to Mr. James Zeigler, director of the Holy Spirit Research Center at Oral Roberts University, who provided me with audio and videotapes of Oral Roberts and A. A. Allen. Ms. Jeanie Alcott, vice president of Partner Communications with the Oral Roberts Evangelical Association also supplied me with pictures of Oral Roberts. I am grateful to Mr. Glen Gohr, archivist assistant, and Dr. Wayne Warner, director of the Flower Pentecostal Heritage Center of the Assemblies of God, for providing me with pictures of A. A. Allen and Aimee Semple McPherson. Ms. Carol Gray, executive director of the Kathryn Kuhlman Foundation in Pittsburgh, and Mrs. Earlene Grandstaff, wife of photographer Doug Grandstaff, who often accompanied Kathryn Kuhlman on crusades, granted me permission to use photographs of Kathryn Kuhlman. To these I express my appreciation. I am grateful to Mr. John Simmons and Mr. Tom Murray of the *Charlotte Observer* for providing me with a photograph of Benny Hinn and to Mr. Michael Good, director of photography with the Akron *Beacon Journal* who supplied me with a photograph of Ernest Angley. Ms. Laura Haeford, reporter and former religion editor with the Akron *Beacon Journal* exchanged with me invaluable data on Ernest Angley as did Mr. and Mrs. Gary Fouse of Akron, Ohio, without whom chapter five could not have been completed. Mr. Pearry Green, minister of the Tucson Tabernacle in Tucson, Arizona granted me permission to use a photograph, audiotapes, and videotapes of William Branham. To him I am thankful. I extend my appreciation to Dr. Dennis Bailey, executive secretary of the Religious Communication Association, for providing me with permission to quote freely from articles that I previously published in the *Journal of Communication and Religion*. Finally, to the folks at my home institution, the University of North Carolina at Wilmington, I offer a special note of thanks. Reference librarians Louise Jackson and Donna Gunter were always willing to offer a hand in helping me uncover some esoteric information. Ms. Mickey Elliot, circulation librarian, contributed from her personal collection of materials on Benny Hinn. To these ladies I owe so much. To my good friend and colleague in the Department of Communication Studies, Dr. Lou Buttino, I extend special thanks for the hours he spent reading and commenting on each chapter as they would emerge from my word processor. His insights were always constructive and his inspiration always seemed to come at the right moment. In spite of the help I have received from the above individuals, I, alone, am ultimately responsible for whatever good or bad comes from this book.

Introduction

BACKGROUND

This book is about rhetoric. To the uninitiated, the term rhetoric is ambiguous and confusing. For some it symbolizes empty speech and conjures up the image of a lying politician bent on securing votes by promising more than he or she is able, or intends, to deliver.

One of the earliest definitions of rhetoric is offered by the Greek philosopher Aristotle, who wrote on the subject over twenty-four hundred years ago. He suggests that it is "the faculty of observing in any given case the available means of persuasion" (*Rhetoric* 24). In the same vein, contemporary scholars Brock, Scott, and Chesebro define rhetoric as "the human effort to induce cooperation through the use of symbols" (14). Although they admit that this definition "gives rise to troublesome questions of inclusion and exclusion," (14) at the bottom is the notion of social influence or persuasion. Rhetoric, then, involves symbolic inducement, or persuasion through symbols, whether verbal or nonverbal, spoken or written.

Rhetorical critics are those who study the persuasive discourse of others, be they politicians, pundits, or preachers. Andrews suggests that rhetorical criticism is "the systematic process of illuminating and evaluating the products of human activity" (4). In Andrew's view, rhetorical criticism asks, "What potential did the message have to influence what audience or audiences in what ways?" (6).

In perhaps the most quoted passage dealing with rhetorical criticism, Wichelns, in his 1925 seminal essay "The Literary Criticism of Oratory," suggests that rhetorical criticism "is not concerned with permanence nor yet with beauty. It is concerned with effect. It regards a speech as a communication to a specific audience, and holds its business to be the analysis and appreciation of the orator's method of imparting his ideas to his hearers" (Wichelns 54). Black, in his classic book *Rhetorical Criticism: A Study in Method* offers a similar idea when he explains that rhetorical criticism focuses on persuasive speakers or discourse, that is, persuasive in intent, not necessarily in accomplishment. "Essays in rhetorical criticism," argues Black, "focus on persuasive speakers or discourses, and the weight of the rhetorical tradition too falls in that direction. Consequently, we are obliged to conclude that the subject matter of rhetorical criticism is persuasive discourse" (14).

Although the specific goals of rhetorical criticism vary from critic to critic, the ultimate aim of all critics is to shed light on discourse. Walter points out, for example, that since speeches are such powerful social forces, a listener needs "profound and searching insight into the speeches he hears." Society needs to know the "truth or falsity" of a message, and since society is in need of these insights, it needs rhetorical critics ("On the Varieties of Rhetorical Criticism" 160).

Auer contends that the purpose of a rhetorical critic is threefold: (1) to report what happens or happened, (2) to analyze or interpret the communication event, and (3) ultimately to judge or evaluate the effects of a rhetorical event (3–4). Likewise, Rosenfield believes the end purpose of the critic is to appraise or evaluate the discourse. To support this notion, Rosenfield quotes Black: "At the culmination of the critical process is the evaluation of the discourse or of its author. . . . There is . . . no criticism without appraisal . . ." (154).

In his essay "On the Varieties of Rhetorical Criticism," after calling for the development of explicit rhetorical theories like Aristotle's as found in his *Rhetoric*, Otis Walter suggests that scholars not overlook the construction of implicit rhetorical theories as well. He notes that although only a few societies throughout history, such as those of the Greco-Roman and Western civilizations, have ever produced explicit rhetorical treatises, all cultures and subcultures contain an implied—

or to borrow Walter's term—an "implicit" rhetorical theory. An implicit theory is "a theory of how communication ought to proceed, and what is appropriate, dangerous, unusual, or saintly" (169). These "unexpressed" theories of communication "exist in all cultures and subcultures" and are "the distinctive marks that stamp one as a taciturn New Hampshire farmer, as a child of the slums, as a product of university education, as an introvert or an extrovert" (169–70). In other words, what does a New Hampshire farmer say and how does he say it? How does a child of the ghetto talk? What are the remarks of a person with a university education? What discourse separates introverts from extroverts?

Extending the list further, we might just as appropriately ask, what is the implicit rhetorical profile of twentieth-century American healing revivalists, often popularly referred to as faith healers? Since faith healing has been such a pervasive religious phenomenon in this country throughout the twentieth century, replete with its own rich rhetorical tradition, and since many people not a part of this subculture do not understand it, it beckons us to delve into its mysteries in an attempt to unravel them.

According to Walter, implicit or "unexpressed" theories of rhetoric are valuable because they "reveal the ways in which such groups both communicate and evaluate the communication they hear" (170). Hence, the value of an implicit rhetorical theory of twentieth-century faith healing lies not only in its ability to explain how healing revivalists communicate in general but also in its ability to shed light on why this discourse—and by extension the concept of miraculous healing—has been (and continues to be) so favorably received by millions throughout this century.

PURPOSE

My purpose in this book is not to examine every healing revivalist of the twentieth century. Instead, I have tried to focus primarily on the most well-known, albeit sometimes controversial individuals. These include Aimee Semple McPherson, William Branham, Oral Roberts, Asa Alonso (A. A.) Allen, Ernest Angley, Kathryn Kuhlman, and Benny Hinn. My purpose is not to say everything there is to say about these people but to give the reader a thorough sampling of their discourse. In several cases, entire books about these people already exist, most of which are biographical in nature. My aim, instead, is to allow the reader to experience vicariously what it might have been like to sit in the audience of any of the above healers. What did they look like? How did they act? What did they say? How did they symbolically induce their listeners? To whom were they speaking? How did their audiences receive them? My purpose is to analyze faith healing as its own genre of rhetoric. What is it, in other words, that we can say about faith healing as a body of discourse? In order to answer that question, we must first examine individual orators in isolation.

I begin the discussion of faith healing in chapter one with the flamboyant, popular Aimee Semple McPherson who made her mark in the 1920s and 1930s before dying in 1944. Chapter two focuses on William Branham, who, along with Oral Roberts, was immensely popular immediately following World War II. Had Branham not died untimely from injuries sustained in a car wreck in 1965, it is likely that more people in the twentieth century would have known of him just as they know of Oral Roberts. In chapter three, I focus on Oral Roberts. Although much has already been written about Roberts, largely by Harrell in his 600 page biography, I felt that any book on twentieth-century faith healing would be incomplete without a chapter on him. He is probably the single most popular faith healer of the entire twentieth century. Chapter four deals with the highly controversial figure A. A. Allen, who was very popular in the 1950s. Chapter five looks at the popular evangelist Ernest Angley, who began his Akron ministry in 1954 and has been holding "miracle services" ever since. Chapter six addresses the female faith healer Kathryn Kuhlman, who, although began preaching in the 1920s, held her first miracle service in 1948 and was internationally famous until her death in 1976. Chapter seven features the contemporary and popular faith healer Benny Hinn, who was influenced by Kathryn Kuhlman. After elucidating the rhetoric of each of these individuals in isolation, I draw conclusions in chapter eight about the rhetoric of twentieth-century faith healing in general. Then I compare their healings to the types one reads about in the synoptic gospels. How are they alike? How are they different? Does it really matter?

APPROACH

Brock, Scott, and Chesebro define rhetorical genres as "groups of discourses which share substantive, stylistic, and situational characteristics" (335). Stated differently, "In the discourses that form a genre, similar substantive and stylistic strategies are used to encompass situations perceived as similar by the responding rhetors" (335). Campbell and Jamieson suggest that "a genre is composed of a constellation of recognizable forms bound together by an internal dynamic" or a "synthetic core in which certain significant rhetorical elements, e.g., a system of belief, lines of argument, stylistic choices, and the perception of the situation are fused into an indivisible whole" (21).

Both Campbell and Jamieson (21) and Brock, Scott, and Chesebro suggest that "some genres are established inductively" (337). In these situations, the critic looks at several specific discourses in response to a given similar situation in order to discover what they have in common. The value of generic criticism is that "it permits the critic to generalize beyond the individual event which is constrained by time and place to affinities and traditions across time" (341). It defines "recurrent rhetorical action" that chronologically transcends audiences and rhetors and teaches "about the nature of human communicative response" (342). Cali argues that at least two benefits of conducting generic criticism are that (1) it "provides a history of communication rules" and (2) it sheds light on "social or cultural reasoning" (13).

The potential consequences surrounding the discourse of faith healers are too dangerous to ignore. If it is true that an individual can receive a personal miraculous healing, then does it not make sense to invite the diseased and afflicted to attend an assembly like those we will discuss momentarily where they could receive an instantaneous cure? What individual in his or her right mind would not want to be healed? If, on the other hand, after careful consideration, we conclude that there is little, if any, validity to the claims that faith healers make, we cannot (nor should not) merely pass them off as uninformed, benign preachers who do not know any better but who, nonetheless, should be listened to because, after all, they are preaching sincerely. In the final analysis, the rhetorical critic must pass judgment, and sometimes this judgment is incisive.

In writing this book, I have attempted to follow the lead of rhetorical scholar Sonja Foss. She explains that when attempting to establish a genre, the rhetorical critic should proceed along four lines. First, critics note similar situations "removed from each other in time and place" that produce "similar rhetorical responses." These situations should not serve as preconceived notions that assume a genre but should serve merely as an initial "prod" to critics to determine whether a genre really exists. Second, critics collect several samples of discourse from similar rhetorical situations "preferably from various historical periods." Third, critics analyze the rhetorical artifacts for "substantive and stylistic features." Foss points out that critics are not bound by any particular method of analysis. Instead, they allow the artifact to "suggest" substantive and/or stylistic similarities and differences that are the most salient. These could include, but are not limited to, "metaphors, images, sentence structure, failure to enact arguments," "adoption of a belligerent tone or use of ambiguous terminology," etc. Finally, critics "formulate the organizing principle that captures the essence of the strategies common to the sample collected." The labeling of the organizing principle may occur simultaneously with the delineation of the substantive and stylistic commonalties of the rhetorical acts analyzed (229–31).

In my research, I analyzed countless hours of audiotapes and videotapes. In some cases, like that of McPherson and Branham, few videotapes exist. Therefore, I had to rely largely on audiotapes and printed materials, such as collections of sermons, books written by the revivalists themselves, or magazines and other literature published by their organizations. In the final analysis, there was more than enough material on any given faith healer for one to develop a proper understanding of his or her rhetorical methods.

In analyzing the discourse of faith healers, I followed no prescribed plan, adhering instead to the advice of theorists Black and Klyn. Black argues that "critical method is too personally expressive to be systematized" (x). Likewise, Klyn reasons, "rhetorical criticism . . . only means intelligent writing about works of rhetoric . . . in whatever way the critic can manage it." He believes that criticism "does not imply a prescriptive mode of writing [or] any categorical structure of judgment . . . (147)." Therefore, the rhetorical critic should be "uninhibited methodologically and free to use his mind as well—perhaps as unconventionally—as he can" (156). Campbell and Jamieson suggest that "a concern with form and genre does not prescribe a critical methodology" (27). In light of these remarks, I merely allowed the rhetorical artifacts to speak to me, noting the most salient features of each faith healer. As it turned out, much of what is discussed could easily be classified around the five classical canons of rhetoric probably cataloged by Cicero in the *Rhetorica Ad Herennium*. These include inventio (development), dispositio (organization), elecutio (style), memoria (memory), and pronunciatio (delivery) (see also Golden, Berquist, and Coleman 1989, 13). In most cases, I have consciously chosen not to use these terms as center headings in each chapter to avoid a formulaic, cookie-cutter approach. In spite of this, many chapters wound up looking similar anyway. In most chapters, after providing some background on each faith healer, I discussed the nature of their audiences. Then I focused on their lines of argument (i.e. inventio or development), after which I discussed their style and delivery. In between I made mention of how organized their sermons were.

SIGNIFICANCE

As long as people continue to become ill or to be born with physical and emotional maladies and as long as individuals like those covered in this book proclaim miraculous deliverance from such ailments, I believe books like this one need to be written. While I do not claim to have the answer to every question involving faith and healing, I believe some answers are too obvious to be overlooked. A close analysis of the discourse of healing revivalists is a fruitful starting point in trying to understand how they induce cooperation in their hearers and why faith healing has been so attractive throughout the twentieth century.

There is a second reason I believe this study is important. If I am successful in establishing the rhetorical parameters of faith healers, not only should this book help us to become better consumers of faith healing discourse, but it will also help to delineate this genre from other forms of Pentecostal or charismatic preaching as well as from fundamentalists' rhetoric in general. While there may be a number of similarities between these groups, I believe that faith healing is its own genre and should not be confused with either fundamentalists' rhetoric or the rhetoric of other Pentecostal groups such as snake handlers or contemporary Pentecostal televangelists who don't practice healings per se. These rhetorics, while perhaps close, are not necessarily the same.

I have often thought that the words of hostile witnesses who accused the apostle Peter of being a disciple of Christ on the night of Christ's betrayal as recorded in Matthew 26:73 are appropriate to describe twentieth-century American faith healers—"for thy speech betrayeth thee" (King James Version). This became the basis for the title of chapter eight. Simply put, my contention is that the speech of faith healers betrays them. It marks them for what they are. One can listen to an individual preach and know within a short time whether that individual practices faith healing. Many faith healers employ the same language. Many of them have similar preaching and healing styles. And, most of them apply the same arguments and evidence. In the pages that follow, my aim is to explain how.

REFERENCES

Andrews, James R. *The Practice of Rhetorical Criticism*. New York: Macmillan Publishing Co., 1983.

Aristotle. *The Rhetoric*. Trans. W. Rhys Roberts. New York: Modern Library, 1954.

Auer, J. Jeffrey. "What Does a Rhetorical Critic Do?" Unpublished essay, 1981.

Black, Edwin. *Rhetorical Criticism: A Study in Method*. 1965. Madison, WI: University of Wisconsin Press, 1978.

Brock, Bernard L., Robert L. Scott, and James W. Chesebro. *Methods of Rhetorical Criticism: A Twentieth-Century Perspective*. 3rd ed. Detroit: Wayne State University Press, 1989.

Cali, Dennis D. *Generic Criticism of American Public Address*. Dubuque, IA: Kendall/Hunt, 1996.

Campbell, Karlyn Kohrs, and Kathleen Hall Jamieson, eds. *Form and Genre: Shaping Rhetorical Action*. Falls Church, VA: Speech Communication Association, n.d.

Cicero. *Rhetorica Ad Herennium*. Trans. Harry Caplan. Cambridge, MA: Harvard University Press, 1981.

Foss, Sonja K. *Rhetorical Criticism: Exploration and Practice*. Prospect Heights, IL: Waveland Press, 1989.

Golden, James L., Goodwin F. Berquist, and William E. Coleman. *The Rhetoric of Western Thought*. 4th ed. Dubuque, IA: Kendall/Hunt, 1989.

Harrell, David Edwin. *Oral Roberts: An American Life*. Bloomington, IN: Indiana University Press, 1985.

Klyn, Mark S. "Toward a Pluralistic Rhetorical Criticism." *Essays on Rhetorical Criticism*. Ed. Thomas R. Nilsen. New York: Random House, 1968. 146–58.

Rosenfield, Lawrence W. "The Anatomy of Critical Discourse." *Methods of Rhetorical Criticism: A Twentieth-Century Perspective*. Eds. Robert L. Scott and Bernard L. Brock. New York: Harper and Row, 1972. 131–57.

Walter, Otis M. "On the Varieties of Rhetorical Criticism." *Essays on Rhetorical Criticism*. Ed. Thomas R. Nilsen. New York: Random House, 1968. 158–77.

Wichelns, Herbert A. "The Literary Criticism of Oratory Rpt." *Methods of Rhetorical Criticism: A Twentieth-Century Perspective*. Eds. Robert L. Scott and Bernard L. Brock. New York: Harper and Row, 1972. 27–60.

Aimee Semple McPherson, ca. 1920. Courtesy of The Flower Pentecostal Heritage Center. Reprinted with permission.

CHAPTER ONE

They Called Her "Sister": Aimee Semple McPherson

Of all religious leaders in twentieth-century American Christendom, perhaps none was more popular and influential in his or her day than the auburn-haired, Canadian-born farmgirl who rose to stardom as a faith healer and evangelist extraordinaire by the name of Aimee Semple McPherson. Her career—relatively short compared to the longevity of such notables as Billy Graham and Oral Roberts—lasted approximately three and a half decades. During this time, however, she preached and ministered to millions of individuals who were drawn to her magnetic personality, some merely out of curiosity, others out of total devotion. At the height of her career in the early 1920s, she and her contemporary Billy Sunday were, without doubt, the two most popular evangelists in America.

Edith Blumhofer, one of several McPherson biographers, rightly refers to her as "an American sensation" who possessed an "unwavering commitment to divine healing" (1, 4–5). In fact, some believe that McPherson may have been "the greatest faith healer of all time" (Reynolds 35). Writing in *Harper's Monthly Magazine* in 1927 from eye-witness observation, journalist Sarah Comstock suggests that McPherson's influence as an evangelist and faith healer "is incredible, that it carries as that of few evangelists has ever carried, that she is today [sic] one of the most amazing phenomena of power in this feverish, power-insane United States" (16). Similarly, writing in 1929, Budlong suggests that "no figure in revivalism is so interesting and significant as the Reverend Aimee Semple McPherson" (737). While McPherson had her share of enemies, the likes of which eventually included members of her own family, "Sister," as her followers affectionately referred to her, was a godsend for millions, offering salvation, relieving suffering, and bringing hope to those who had all but resigned themselves to a life of pain and misery.

"Sister Aimee" was born to James and Minnie Pearce Kennedy on October 9, 1890, on a farm in Salford, Ontario, about five miles south of Ingersol, where she grew up. Her father, fifty years old when Aimee was born, was a devout Methodist. Her fifteen-year-old mother was a staunch member of the Salvation Army (see McLoughlin; Bahr; Austin; McWilliams; Thomas; Blumhofer; and Epstein for biographical information on McPherson).

Although Aimee's early life in and around the Salvation Army helped to prepare her for her own ministry, much of what she learned theologically can be attributed to her first husband. On August 12, 1908, a few years before she would begin her career as an itinerant evangelist, seventeen-year-old Aimee Kennedy married a redheaded Irishman named Robert James Semple, a handsome Pentecostal preacher who had come to Ingersol to hold a revival. It was Semple who was directly responsible for Aimee's conversion to Pentecostalism in February 1908 and subsequent teachings on the baptism of the Holy Ghost and gifts of the Spirit.

Shortly after their marriage they left for India and China for missionary work. While in China, on September 17, 1910, daughter Roberta Star Semple was born, one month after Robert Semple's untimely death as a result of malaria. In January 1911, in response to what she believed was a call from God, Aimee returned to the United States.

In 1912 she married Harold Stewart McPherson in Chicago. Through marriage to McPherson, Aimee became an American citizen. On March 23, 1913, she gave birth to her second child and only son Rolf Kennedy McPherson. Within a couple of years, in June 1915, Aimee, with two children in tow, left Harold McPherson, who was unresponsive to her unquenchable desire to reenter the ministry. Harold preferred Aimee to stay at home and raise the children while Aimee, who wanted nothing more than to proclaim the gospel to others, was chafing under such domestic responsibilities. Eventually their marriage ended in divorce in April 1921. Harold sued on grounds of desertion.

In June 1915, with Harold McPherson at least temporarily out of her way, Aimee could pursue what she firmly believed was another call from God to harvest souls. Even before her divorce from Harold McPherson in 1921, Aimee had begun to hold meetings. She held her first revival in Mount Forest, Ontario in August 1915. Between 1916 and 1918 she had preached in Boston and on Long Island as well as in other major cities and had toured Florida twice. Between 1918 and 1923 "Sister Aimee" crisscrossed the United States and Canada some eight or nine times holding close to forty revivals in the largest cities. It was not until 1921 that she decided to build a permanent tabernacle in Los Angeles, which would house the ministry of her recently founded denomination, "The Church of the Foursquare Gospel." She completed the 5,300 seat Angelus Temple in 1923 where she would eventually preach over twenty sermons per week and start radio KFSG (Kalling Four Square Gospel) in February 1924. McPherson was the first evangelist to own and operate her own radio station. On December 7, 1925, she opened a six-story school near Angelus Temple known as the Lighthouse of International Foursquare Evangelism, or more simply to McPherson and those in her organization, L.I.F.E. Bible College.

Trouble soon rocked McPherson's ministry. On May 18, 1926, she was reported missing after taking a swim at Ocean Park, California. Many believed she had drowned until she showed up at Agua Prieta, Mexico just across the border from Douglas, Arizona on June 23, 1926. She told of how she had been kidnapped by three individuals known only as "Rose," "Steve," and "Jake." Witnesses surfaced, however, suggesting that they had seen her at a motel in Carmel, California with Kenneth Ormiston, a married man and former radio engineer at KFSG. On September 16, 1926, McPherson was officially charged with obstructing justice and corruption of morals. On January 10, 1927, after several months of negative press and emotionally charged court proceedings, Los Angeles District Attorney Asa Keyes dropped the charges against McPherson. It appears that he did not have sufficient evidence to win the case, although some have suggested that he may have been party to a $30,000 bribe. Ultimately, Keyes would spend time in San Quentin prison for accepting a bribe in an unrelated case (McWilliams 50–80).

On September 13, 1931, at the age of forty, McPherson, who had grown desperately lonely through the years, married twenty-nine-year-old David Hutton, an overweight, gap-toothed baritone she had chosen to play the lead role in her illustrated sermon "The Iron Furnace." Problems soon surfaced when a woman named Myrtle Hazel St. Pierre sued Hutton for $200,000 for breaking his promise to marry her. Two other women came forward to announce that they intended to file similar charges. Hutton, who apparently married more out of a desire to boost his career than out of love for Aimee, filed for a divorce which was granted him on March 1, 1934, just three short years after a stormy and publicly controversial marriage which, to Aimee, must have seemed like an eternity (Blumhofer 319–23, 41).

After several years of poor health, McPherson was feeling well enough to travel to Oakland, California in September 1944 to preach at the dedication services of a newly opened branch of the Church of the Foursquare Gospel. The night of Tuesday, September 26, she retired to her hotel room after preaching a sermon to spend some private time with her son Rolf. The next morning around ten o'clock when Rolf called on her, he found her unconscious. He also found several pills strewn on the bed and floor around it. By noon, McPherson was pronounced dead, ruled as "shock and respiratory failure from an accidental overdose of barbital compound and a kidney ailment." Ironically, her funeral was held on her birthday on October 9, 1944, at Angelus Temple. She was buried in Forest Lawn Cemetery in Los Angeles (Blumhofer 375–79). That year McPherson had applied for a television license and probably would have succeeded in using this new medium had she lived (Hadden and Swann). Harrell notes that, upon McPherson's death, American Pentecostalism had lost its most popular public figure (*All Things Are Possible* 16). *Time* magazine referred to her as "the most spectacular U.S. evangelist since Billy Sunday" (58, 60).

No one can doubt the incredible success that Aimee Semple McPherson enjoyed as an evangelist and faith healer within the first third of this century. Not only had she won a gold medal as a school girl for her "magnificent oratorical power," but she had won millions of souls to God (Blumhofer 153). In the words of Comstock, "the curious would like to know how, in popular parlance, the lady puts it over" (16).

Our purpose in this chapter, and in those that follow, is to address this question from a rhetorical standpoint. What was it about Mc-

Pherson's preaching that appealed to the masses? More importantly, how was it that she was able to sell the notion of faith healing to others, to symbolically induce them to believe? How, to quote Worthington, did she hold "spellbound the crowd of her followers who are unable to penetrate the mystery of how she does what she does" (550)? If we hope to attain answers to the above questions regarding McPherson—or any other faith healer within the twentieth century for that matter—we must first understand the nature of the audiences to whom they spoke.

McPHERSON'S FOLLOWERS

McLoughlin suggests that McPherson appealed "to people of little education and small means" who no longer found "inspiration" in the "old evangelical tradition" of their various denominations (213). Austin describes how migrants from the Midwestern "dust bowl" during the Depression years came to Los Angeles "with no money, no prospects, [and] no education" (48). Nine out of ten people in Aimee's audiences were converted out of orthodox Protestantism. By and large, they were immigrants from farms and small towns in the Midwest (McWilliams 59). These individuals were fundamentalists with little education (Ebeling 154). Blumhofer describes McPherson's audiences as "poor" (122), "multidenominational" (389), "blue-collar working class," and "emotionally unstable" (391). Those who supported McPherson, contends Blumhofer, were "plain folks" (289, 329) and "ordinary people" (230), who lacked "social status and religious influence" (209). Budlong labels McPherson's followers "poor," "undernourished," and "maladjusted" (737). Comstock calls them "more or less ignorant, credulous, and susceptible to cheap emotionalism" (15). Everywhere Aimee preached, the crowds were the same.

Commenting on those who followed her, McPherson herself once remarked, "I bring consolation to the great middle class, leaving those below to the Salvation Army, and those above to themselves" (Epstein 330). She saw her mission as "preaching to the poor . . . of Jesus' soon coming" (Blumhofer 209).

Let us not overlook the fact that, like all faith healers of the twentieth century, McPherson responded to the maladies of the people of her day. In fact, those with physical ailments frequently flocked to McPherson's services, whether held in large auditoriums, tents, or

Angelus Temple. In fact, Wednesday afternoons and Saturday nights were devoted to faith healing at Angelus Temple. Epstein points out that while later in her career McPherson tried to "diffuse the public's interest" in faith healing, she never really abandoned it (399). Healings were deferred to the end of services when individuals would line up one by one to await their turn for Aimee to anoint their foreheads with olive oil and lay her hands on them in order for them to receive a miraculous cure. For hours on end and long into the night, "Sister" would cast out demons, which she believed brought pain and suffering, and pronounce healings on all who had enough faith to believe (Blumhofer 215; Epstein 178, 210; *Divine Healing Sermons* 59, 80–82).

That McPherson understood the desperation of her followers is evident in many of her sermons. In her sermon "Seven Keys to Power," for example, she perceptively suggested to many in her audience that God will open "the legions and the handcuffs and the wheelchair and the hospital door for you." "Invalid, sick, shut in the dungeon of despair—all you need to do is ask him. He'll give you the key." In her sermon "This is My Task," she disclosed that part of her job as an evangelist was to help people become well: "You have no business being sick. Everyone of you should get well and get up and go to work . . . and help send the gospel out."

Newspaper accounts of McPherson's audiences occasionally described them as "a mass of twisted, suffering, misshapen humanity" (Epstein 196). San Jose's *Mercury Herald* on one occasion reported, "The number of invalids and hopeful sick who gather at every meeting has increased until the front row beside the altar resembles a great convalescing ward. In wheel chairs, on stretchers and crutches, others hobbling and almost unable to walk, they rise to their feet at every prayer . . ." (Epstein 221).

After visiting one of McPherson's healing services, Worthington described her followers as "good people with toil-worn hands and heavy faces, unlearned and unskilled in things of the mind, but great in the realm of feeling and deeply moved by what they see and hear" (550). He argued, "It does not occur to these simple people to ask if what they see may be something different from what takes place or if what they feel may always be trustworthy evidence of what is going on. It is evident that without such an audience as this Aimee Semple McPherson would be lost" (550).

When we analyze the preaching of Aimee Semple McPherson, we

realize that there are a number of rhetorical factors in combination with each other that made her persuasive to her desperate followers. In other words, as with any other faith healer in this study, no one element in and of itself can account for her success. Let us begin, therefore, by focusing on one of her most salient rhetorical attributes—her narrative style.

McPHERSON'S NARRATIVE STYLE

When listening to the preaching of Aimee Semple McPherson, it does not take long to recognize that much of what she preached was presented as one long story or as a series of extended stories and anecdotes clustering around a common spiritual theme. Schuetz points out that, generally, McPherson's storytelling fell into one of two categories: allegorical or autobiographical. Allegorical stories were stories about everyday events that taught a spiritual lesson. Autobiographical stories, on the other hand, were those about the speaker herself, and were intended to "help define the community and establish the credibility of the storyteller" (31).

Perhaps the best example of autobiographical stories is seen in McPherson's sermon "From Milkpail to Pulpit," in which she recounted the story of her life from her beginnings in Ontario, Canada where she fell in love with Robert Semple, was converted and called to the ministry, and returned home from a heart-wrenching missionary trip to China. This was not really a sermon in the traditional sense in which a preacher offers three or four main points around a common thesis and supports them, although McPherson often did this. Instead, it was simply a retelling of selected events in her life. Nonetheless, it provided interesting information, and McPherson was able to capture and maintain her audiences' attention with this type of preaching.

Most sermons McPherson preached, however, were not one long story about her life or the life of any other person for that matter. Yet, her sermons were still packed with illustration after illustration, some taken from her personal life, some taken from the Bible, and some taken from everyday events. After listening to her preach, Bissell described her sermon as "a handful of proof-texts loosely strung together with commonplace illustrations" (127). These illustrations or narratives, based either on biblical characters or everyday events, are examples of what Schuetz calls allegorical. One of the best examples of this is found in her sermon "Livewire." In this sermon McPherson opened with a humorous story about being shocked by an electric blanket one night while sleeping. Much to the delight of her audience, she suggested that being shocked felt as if a Bengal tiger had jumped on her. The electric blanket "shot me across the room" against the wall before her secretary entered excitedly, asking "What's the matter?" "All I could say was that, that, that, that, that," stuttered McPherson, retelling her harrowing experience in dramatic linguistic style as her audience roared with laughter. The spiritual implication, which McPherson eventually made, was that "God's power is a live-wire! And these are livewire services" where "marvelous healings" take place.

Later in the same sermon McPherson humorously told of a pelican who flew across Glendale Boulevard in Echo Park, where Angelus Temple is located, into a power line, knocking out all of the electricity and bringing the streetcars to a grinding halt. As was often her approach, she told the Biblical stories of Nadab and Abihu, Uzzah, the man in the Old Testament who steadied the ark, "the three Hebrew children" Shadrach, Meshach, and Abednego, Daniel in the lions' den, Ananias and Sapphiras, and Saul on the road to Damascus. In keeping with the theme of "Livewire," all of these stories were intended to illustrate the power of God and, hence, to convince her audience of the miraculous.

In her sermon "Seven Keys to Power," a well-organized, step by step approach to finding "the key to paradise," McPherson typically told story after story to support various assertions. These stories ranged from that of a burglar who stole the purse of a lady at a birthday party, to staying in a hotel in Colorado where hundreds of keys hung on the wall, to a prisoner talking the daughter of a prison warden out of her keys, among others. One story that McPherson often repeated was that of a Santa Monica man who "fell over the palisades" in the dark. Fearing he would drown in the ocean if he let go, and not knowing how far he would fall, he held on until he could hold on no more. Finally, at the point of exhaustion he slipped and fell only "three and a half inches." "If you give in to God," reminds McPherson, "friends, you won't have far to fall" ("Divine Healing"). Suffice it to say, stories like these were inextricably woven into the preaching of Aimee Semple McPherson, which made her appealing to listen to. But the question is: From what does McPherson's storytelling draw its enormous rhetorical power?

Relying in part on Fisher's narrative theory, Schuetz reveals that

McPherson's stories moved her audiences because they contained three key ingredients: "narrative probability, narrative fidelity, and standard of moral judgment."

Narrative probability means that the stories told are "coherent accountings of actions, attitudes, and values between the storyteller and the audience." Schuetz suggests, in other words, that millions of people trusted McPherson's "representations and interpretations of reality" (33–34).

Narrative fidelity means that the stories "ring true" with the audience. Stated differently, audiences have had or have known others who have had similar experiences in their own lives (Schuetz 33–34). Thus, for example, stories about being shocked by electric blankets or power being knocked out by flying birds ring true for audiences. People can relate to these events because they have experienced them. Even McPherson herself occasionally reminded her audiences that they had experienced what she was telling. For instance, once she remarked how everyone had, at some point in their life, gone through a tunnel and that when doing so did not "shutter and shake" because they knew there was an opening at the other end. She then made the analogy that Jesus died "for us." Jesus, in effect, built the tunnel ("Many Members, One Body").

Standard of moral judgment means that stories are successful in that they teach what is morally right and wrong by whether Biblical or contemporary people succeeded or failed in their actions (Schuetz 33–34). Thus, for instance, when audiences listened to McPherson enumerate the foibles and fiascos of Biblical characters, they understood which actions were sanctioned by God and which were not. It was in these three ways that McPherson's stories were powerful rhetorical devices in attracting and inducing audiences to accept what she preached.

As has already been pointed out in numerous historical works about McPherson, she was particularly successful because of another form of storytelling—the illustrated sermon, which she presented on Sunday nights at Angelus Temple. These were generally allegorical stories that McPherson narrated while actors on stage acted out the roles of various characters in the sermon. Even preacher McPherson herself occasionally donned a costume and assumed a role.

One of her most famous illustrated sermons is the "Cat and the Canary," religious theatre about how the devil, illustrated by the cat, is always trying to lure Christians, depicted by the canary, into his paws. Blumhofer tells us that it was Evangeline Booth, the eighth and final child of William Booth, founder of the Salvation Army in London, England in 1865, who originally developed the illustrated sermon. McPherson adapted and improved upon this form of preaching after moving to Angelus Temple (50). Her illustrated sermons were so successful that actor Charlie Chaplin, who periodically slipped into Angelus Temple incognito to watch them, once remarked to McPherson, "Half your success is due to your magnetic appeal, half due to the props and lights" (Epstein 351).

McPherson gives us some insight into why she preached the way she did when she remarked, "Right at the outset, there was borne in upon me the realization that the methods so often used to impart religion were too archaic, too sedate and too lifeless ever to capture the interest of the throngs. . . . So I developed methods which have brought hundreds of thousands to meetings who otherwise would never have come" (*In The Service of the King* 152). Looking back upon all of the people who flocked to McPherson's services and who eventually came forward to be saved and/or to be healed, who would disagree that the storytelling methods she employed were successful? Butler summarizes the effectiveness of these methods when he suggests that "followers caught Christian truth in . . . fascinating and powerful stories . . . ; before their very eyes and ears, McPherson transformed dry theology into the drama of life in all its agony, pageantry, and, yes, in its silliness too. In McPherson, faith *was* narrative" (145).

McPHERSON'S RELIANCE ON SCRIPTURE

In addition to her captivating style of preaching, *what* McPherson articulated equally contributed to her success as a faith healer. Given the fact that her audience was composed predominantly of fundamentalist Christians, who relied heavily on a literal interpretation of the Bible, we are not surprised to find that McPherson, too, greatly emphasized scripture in an effort to convince her followers that they could receive a miraculous cure. Since to McPherson, "God's word is true," one needed merely to have faith, to "put your faith into actions" because "faith without works is dead." It says so in the Bible, she taught. ("Power of Faith"; "How to Receive a Healing" in *Divine Healing Sermons* 71).

In her sermon "How to Receive a Healing," McPherson raised the question, "What should be the attitude of the church toward divine healing?" "There is only one way in which to rightfully answer this question," she responded, "and that is from the Word of God" (*Divine Healing Sermons*, 98–99).

Certainly McPherson's favorite passage was Hebrews 13:8, a commonly employed verse of other faith healers as we will notice in subsequent chapters. "Brother, I tell you," said McPherson, "the Lord is the same yesterday, today, and forever. He's able to save and heal tonight" ("Seven Sneezes of Shumen"). Hebrews 13:8 was such a favorite verse of McPherson that she had it inscribed on the front of Angelus Temple, as well as over the proscenium on the inside, and across the front of every Four Square Gospel Church across the country. In effect, Hebrews 13:8 was McPherson's scriptural trademark. Blumhofer reminds us that McPherson read Hebrews 13:8 "with conviction, carrying the text toward its simplest, most logical conclusions, and the crowds loved it" (169).

Other favorite passages were James 5:14 and Isaiah 53:4. After quoting James 5:14, McPherson would sarcastically remark, "I'm sorry my brethren, but this was for yesteryear." After citing Isaiah 53:4, McPherson reminded her followers, "Tonight the Lord Jesus Christ is able to heal you. He's able to raise you up" ("Seven Sneezes of Shumen").

In her sermon "Divine Healing," McPherson made allusion after allusion to scriptures as implicit proof that one could receive a miraculous cure. Before preaching from Luke 13 about a woman who had a "spirit of infirmity for eighteen years," McPherson urged her audience to "Trust God tonight! And believe in His wonderful word" ("Divine Healing"). In the same sermon, she reminded them, "Oh, but thank God in the Bible the Lord healed the lunatic. He healed the blind. He restored their vision." Growing more adamant about receiving miraculous cures, McPherson yelled, "I don't believe it's God's will that you be deaf because the Bible said that Jesus walked up and said, 'Thou deaf spirit come out of him.'" Continuing to rely on the Bible, she pleaded, "The Bible again and again says, 'ought not this woman be loosed whom Satan hath bound?'" ("Divine Healing").

In her sermon on the "Power of Faith," McPherson preached, "God Lives. God's word is true. God's word has been proven." Later she quoted Psalms 103:3 which suggests, "who forgiveth all thine iniquities and healeth all thy diseases." She mentioned Matthew 7:7,

"Ask and ye shall receive, seek and ye shall find, knock and it shall be opened" as evidence that one could receive divine healing. Citing James 5:14 again McPherson preached, "We may pray one for another that we may be healed. You may pray for yourself when you are suddenly falling from a ladder. You may pray for your little baby when suddenly the baby is seized with choaking crup in the middle of the night." In closing this sermon, she prayed to God for "the power and glory of thy manifest" to be "upon us" for "Thou art the same yesterday, today and forever," another reference to Hebrews 13:8 ("Power of Faith").

In one sermon, after reading Psalms 15:1–3, McPherson boldly asserted, "Now you can be healed just like that. That cancer can fall out. I know what I'm talking about. That tumor can go down like a balloon. That trouble of your eyes can be healed" ("Livewire").

In short, to McPherson the key to miraculous cures lay in the fact that the Bible taught it, and she had ample scriptures or prooftexts to back up her claims. Bartow suggests that every "jot and tittle of life and scripture could be interpreted and reinterpreted to support her essential message" (76). He further reveals how she "typically ignored literary and historical context in interpreting texts and accommodated scripture to the view of Jesus that came to her in experience and ecstatic vision. She was her own authority in the sense that God spoke to her directly, telling her what to say and when to say it, what to do and when to do it. And proof that she was not deluded was in her success in attracting sinners . . ." (77–78). Similarly, Bissell argues that McPherson preached a "religious message utterly devoid of sound thinking, loose and insubstantial in its construction, preposterously inadequate in its social implications, but amazingly successful after five years of running, and still going strong, judging from statistics, the infallible appeal of church-men" (158).

Given the fundamentalist nature of her audiences, the fact that McPherson merely alluded to some verse in the Bible was not only expected, but good enough for them to believe in miraculous healing. Her simple followers had neither the expertise nor the inclination to question whether the passages she employed really meant what she interpreted them to mean. Furthermore, since they had heard McPherson use the same verses over and over again to establish her claims, whatever skepticism they may have had—however large it initially might have been—would be suppressed. And so, McPherson's quoting of the Bible became an inducement for her fundamentalist audiences to believe. If they doubted, all they had to do was open the book along with "Sister," and there they could plainly see for themselves in black and white. Who could doubt it?

PRIMARY AND SECONDARY TESTIMONIES

If the authority of the scriptures was not enough to sell the idea of faith healing, those who teeter-tottered on the threshold of doubt would eventually be swayed by "Sister's" use of testimonies. Primary testimonies were those given by McPherson herself about either some healing she saw or about her own personal healing. McPherson often reminded her audiences, "With my own eyes during my ministry I have seen tens of thousands of actual cases of healing that cannot be doubted." She talked of cancers "melt[ing] away," "withered hands" made whole and "bones that were filled with pus . . . instantly healed so that the persons leaped from their wheeling chair or cast aside crutches and walked up and down shout[ing] 'Glory to God.' " She testified of having the "joy of seeing blind eyes opened," of watching people "as their deaf ears were opened," of hearing "the dumb made to speak." "Oh Beloved," she cried, "this is not unusual." "This is the same God who worked when Jesus Christ walked this earth" ("Power of Faith").

McPherson told of a woman who was brought to her services dying "with a great protruding cancer." After the congregation prayed for her, two of McPherson's workers helped her up from her cot. "She rose to her feet," McPherson testified, "and in the presence of the witnesses of this audience walked across the temple platform . . . and down the aisle" ("Seven Sneezes of Shumen"). Here, not only did McPherson use testimony to induce her listeners to believe, but she also appealed to what they themselves had witnessed. This is only one of the many kinds of testimonies McPherson gave about people who were healed in her services (see "Livewire" for others).

When not talking about the cures of other people, "Sister" frequently testified about her own personal healing and calling, when God was tugging at her to preach early in her second marriage to Harold McPherson. "Every day and every night Jesus spoke to my soul, 'Now will you go preach, preach, preach the word of God.' I said Lord, 'I can't go.' I became ill and almost broken and that settled it. Finally, I said yes to God. But not until I'd been taken off of the operating table to die. Finally, as I lay dying, I said, 'yes, Lord, I'll go.' " ("From Milkpail to Pulpit"). McPherson recalled that when she opened her eyes while on her death bed the pain left her after she had said yes to God. "I was able to take deep breaths without the agony which had accompanied the tiniest breath before. I was able to turn over without pain. . . . In two weeks, to the amazement of everyone, I was up and well . . . " (*This is That* 102–03). Dramatic testimony such as this left the listener with the impression that if God can heal someone in such bad shape as McPherson, then He can heal anyone. Moreover, given the fact that McPherson was healed, this was proof positive that God had called her. And, if God had called her, who were they to resist her work of miraculous healing? In this way McPherson's personal testimony persuaded her listeners.

Not only did McPherson employ primary testimony, but she equally applied secondary testimony—the testimony of other people who claimed to be healed (Epstein 168). Among the many who testified was actor Anthony Quinn's grandmother, who once bore witness to God healing her stomach ailment (Epstein 376–78).

In recounting perhaps McPherson's most successful healing campaign in January 1921 in San Diego, Blumhofer writes how invalids testified to being healed and how McPherson observed that those who testified persuaded at least ten other people (Blumhofer 160–61). Son Rolf McPherson suggests that "the testimonies of the people" given in healing services at McPherson's revivals, if written down, "would fill volumes" (R. McPherson). McPherson obviously realized the persuasive impact that one person's story could have on another and allowed the stories to be told frequently in her healing campaigns (Epstein 168). To her it was just one more way to induce her audience. She believed that when people see miracles and hear others' testimonies, "they are jolted from their indifference and complacency. . . . There is nothing left to do but believe" (Blumhofer 166–67).

During a debate over miraculous healings with the Baptist minister Ben M. Bogard in Little Rock in April 1934, McPherson concluded her part of the debate by allowing three people to offer their testimonies of being healed after "Sister" had prayed for them. So strong were these testimonies that when a vote was taken to determine the winner, the audience clearly stood in favor of McPherson and miraculous, divine healings (Blumhofer 326–28). Clearly, McPherson knew the persuasive effect that testimonies have and consciously used them to convince her audiences.

In addition to testimonies told during healing services, like other faith healers to follow, McPherson recorded personal testimonies in her periodical *The Bridal Call*, which she began in June 1917. A famous testimony, for example, was given by actor Johnny Walker who claimed to have been saved and cured of a drug habit and asthma. Another testimony, recorded by Harriet Jordan, McPherson's personal assistant, told of how she was healed of painful intestinal problems during one of McPherson's services (Blumhofer 406–426). One of McPherson's earliest healings and subsequent testimonies to appear in *The Bridal Call* was that of Louise Messnick of Corona, New York who claimed to have been healed of "Arthritis Rheumatism" in 1916 (*This Is That* 128–29).

Rhetorical theorist Richard Weaver points out that testimony is one way an argument becomes compelling. "If we are not in a position to see or examine, but can procure the deposition of some one [sic] who is, the deposition may become the substance of our argument," suggests Weaver. He further reasons that if an argument "is backed by some weighty authority, like the Bible, or can be associated with a great name [strategies that McPherson employed] people may be expected to respond to it in accordance with the veneration they have for these sources. In this way evidence coming from the outside is used to influence attitudes or conduct." Weaver reveals that in the case of testimony, a listener is not being asked "to follow a valid reasoning form but to respond to some presentation of reality. He is being asked to agree with the speaker's interpretation of the world that is" (*Weaver* 209–10).

Testimony probably worked for McPherson for at least three reasons. First, in general, testimony is entertaining. In other words, audiences derive pleasure from either listening to, or reading about, another person's life. And, the more sensational a story is, the more interesting it becomes. Thus, testimony captures an audience's attention. Second, audiences connect psychologically with the person giving the testimony. They have the impression that if something happened to a credible person, it could happen to them as well because both are human and they identify on the basis of similar experiences. Third, testimony becomes particularly persuasive when the listener has a similar need as that fulfilled in a person offering a testimony, especially when an individual has exhausted all other possibilities of having his or her need met. It was in these ways that testimonies probably persuaded individuals in the healing services of Aimee Semple McPherson.

McPHERSON'S HUMILITY AND COMPASSION

Humility and compassion are indispensable assets when appealing to an audience and McPherson exuded them. At least her audiences perceived that she did. McPherson often reminded them, "Friend, I know as God is my judge that I don't amount to anything in myself. I know I'm just a girl from the farm" ("This Is My Task"). She frequently suggested that she was merely "a farmer's daughter" who was raised on "oatmeal porridge" and who walked five miles to school each day ("From Milkpail to Pulpit"). Since most of her followers were transplanted Midwestern farmers, they could identify with McPherson on this ground, if on none other.

After recounting for her listeners her early successes in the ministry, of how sometimes in one service as many as one thousand at a time were saved, she quickly interjected that in spite of this, "I feel I've done so little" ("From Milkpail to Pulpit").

In addition to being self-deprecating, McPherson gave all of the credit for healings to God. She suggested, "Real children of God do not take credit themselves. They place the credit where the credit belongs—upon God. For no man nor woman ever heals the sick. It is Jesus Christ . . . who makes them every whit whole" ("Power of Faith"). In a sermon preached by Rolf McPherson in commemorating his mother's work, Rolf rightly recalled that she "gave to God the credit for all that was accomplished, for she said she could do nothing, but through him all things could be accomplished" (R. McPherson). It was this type of attitude that endeared "Sister" to her followers and helped make her a successful evangelist and faith healer.

Another element that made McPherson popular was the fact that those who sat at her feet were made to feel equal and useful. "Why we're all the same," she suggested, "We all have a heart and we all have tears and we all have sins and we all need a savior and we all need the blood and everyone of us could work for Jesus" ("This Is My Task"). How could McPherson's followers feel useless when she told them that "God loves to use the humble, lowly people. God just loves to take the things that are nought to confound the mighty" ("Many Members, One Body")? Roberta McPherson Salter, Aimee's daughter, recalled how her mother made "everybody" at Angelus Temple believe "that they were somebody important and somebody of service" ("Sister Aimee").

In short, McPherson's audiences felt loved. They felt that Mc-

Pherson genuinely cared for them, that she always had their best interest at heart. Blumhofer underscores this notion when she suggests that McPherson's audiences "came for religion but also for the warm, comfortable, joyous sense of belonging that Sister provided, and she rewarded them with generous doses of both" (231). Because of such goodwill extended to her people, McPherson's ethos was high. Audiences adored her. Howard Courtney, long-time associate of Mc-Pherson and minister of Angelus Temple, believed that she "was a woman who just ran over with compassion" because "she was crushed and bruised and heart broken" herself ("Sister Aimee"). Perhaps such compassion is best seen in her sermon entitled "Divine Healing," where she suggested that God "is a great physician. He's the great healer. Poor man sitting down there holding his head tonight. I know God can touch that eye. . . . Jesus is the great physician. And there's healing in His wings." What suffering individual would not want to believe in the miraculous if approached in such a tender way as Mc-Pherson approached people?

McPHERSON'S ARGUMENT FROM LONGEVITY

"Sister Aimee" was acutely aware that there were always individuals watching her who were skeptical of the miraculous. These she occasionally and directly addressed, attempting to persuade them through argument from longevity. She believed that since she had been conducting healing revivals for so long that her miracles could not possibly be fraudulent. Both she and her works had stood the test of time. Perhaps naively, she believed that she would have been exposed and put out of business had the healings in her revivals been less than what she claimed them to be—miraculous.

Once she articulated the question that seemed to be on many people's minds regarding miraculous cures, "Isn't that rather a fake?" In the very next breath she adamantly reponded, "Absolutely not!" Then she proceeded to argue from longevity. "I've been praying for the sick myself a great many years, sixteen years right here in Angelus Temple. And I know God answers prayer. People are sitting here who used to be epileptic. Epileptics for twenty years instantly healed by using the key of divine healing" ("Seven Keys to Power").

Elsewhere, in addressing her radio audience while preaching in the pulpit of Angelus Temple, Aimee warned, "If you think divine healing is just a freak, you're mistaken. Angelus Temple has been open here sixteen years, praying for the sick. . . . These people by the tens of thousands have been healed and you couldn't keep up anything that was fantastically unreal that long. You'd be found out" ("Livewire").

And so, McPherson believed that "divine healing" was not new to the twentieth century, that it was "as old as the Bible itself," ("Seven Sneezes of Shumen") and that she had been practicing it for a great many years. She believed that if miraculous cures were as tenuous as some people believed them to be, she could not continue being as successful as she was. Implicitly she reminded her skeptics that all they had to do was to look around Angelus Temple and take stock of her success. Proof for the miraculous would be right in front of their eyes.

McPHERSON'S DELIVERY AND OTHER NONVERBAL ELEMENTS

Standing five feet six inches tall and weighing one hundred and fifty pounds, Aimee Semple McPherson was a buxom woman with broad hips and full legs. Her complexion was smooth and her eyes hazel. During the 1920s she wore her long auburn hair piled high in a beehive on her head which accented her round face. After her trial in 1927 Aimee cut her hair, wearing it in tight curls around her head and face. Even in her white nurse's uniform and navy blue cape, which she often wore while preaching, she was still "irresistible" to "at least half the men in America" (Epstein 155–57).

Although certainly not considered gorgeous, when Aimee Semple McPherson stepped into the pulpit there was no doubt that her understated beauty captured the eye. She has been described as "electric, sensual, irresistible," of having her own brand of "sensuous, personal magnetism." Lois Van Cleave, a member of Angelus Temple and a contemporary of Aimee Semple McPherson, recalls how she felt upon seeing "Sister" walk down the ramp of Angelus Temple into the pulpit: "I thought, 'That's the most beautiful woman I ever saw in my life.' " Another eyewitness, Howard Courtney, discloses, "We think she just looked beautiful" ("Sister Aimee").

McWilliams notes that McPherson had two assets "of great potency." One was her voice, the other her "physical vitality." "She suggested sex without being sexually attractive. . . ." She "constantly [emanated] sex" (51). Epstein concurs that she had "an unmistakable sexual energy" (283). Lewis believes that this was one factor that gave her charisma and hence made her rhetorically successful (145–47).

In addition to her physical attractiveness, McPherson's voice was interesting to hear. High pitched—sometimes even shrill—McPherson occasionally spoke so quickly that it became difficult, if not impossible, to understand what she was saying. Audiences were certainly not likely to stray from the sermon due to boredom. Reporters frequently noted her "richly dramatic" voice as a reason for her appeal (Blumhofer 222). One reporter had this to say: "Her voice is a full-throated contralto, and her enunciation in quick speech is excellent. No actress sounds more clearly the last letters or takes advantage of vowels and diphthongs with greater effect" (Blumhofer 303). She often elongated the vowel sound in "God" while accenting the consonants, which "sounded like the beat of a kettledrum" (Epstein 165). Occasionally McPherson rolled her Rs when preaching. For instance, when preaching on the trial of Christ, she dramatically narrated, "I brrrrrring him forth. . . . Crrrrrrucify him" ("Tale of Two Cities"). She probably preached this way from time to time for emphasis, also believing that it would help an audience stay focused on the sermon.

Ebeling adds another dimension to McPherson's delivery—her constant use of one and two syllable words which clarified her ideas and made them understandable to her audiences. These words added imagery and helped hold the listener's attention. Also, her "short," "choppy" sentences, often grouped together, allowed McPherson's preaching to move at a rapid pace and provide maximum interest appeal (157).

Although "Sister" was high pitched and fast talking, she was, at the same time, conversational. Audiences sensed that she was talking *to* them rather than preaching *at* them. Bissell points out that although "Sister" was "rather closely bound to her notes," which protruded from her Bible, she, nonetheless, sounded extemporaneous (127).

She often addressed those in her assemblies as "friends" ("Live-wire"). Even those listening by radio sensed that she was preaching to them when they heard her remark, "Out there by your radio, would you be ready? Lady, I see you sitting there with that cocktail glass in your hands and you, brother, with that cigarette in your hand out there in the radio audience. Would you be ready?" Then, turning to her immediate audience, she pleaded "Would you be ready in the audience of Angelus Temple?" ("The Zero Hour"). Constantly interacting with her audience, McPherson would ask questions: "Everyone here who has ever been healed say amen. How many know you've been healed? Say amen" ("Seven Keys to Power"). Through constant direct address and occasional question raising such as these, McPherson stayed rhetorically connected to her listeners. Blumhofer notes that "Sister" "spoke in the idiom of ordinary people" and involved her audiences by "asking questions, demanding answers, and challenging them to immediate responses" (20). Budlong suggests, "Mrs. McPherson, wheedling, cajoling, admonishing, 'kidding' her vast audience is like a mother with a numerous brood" (738).

Another factor that made McPherson appealing was the mimicry and dialogue that she often employed while preaching. Once, for example, when speaking from Luke 13 about a woman with a spirit of infirmity, McPherson took on a stereotypically low, manly voice when reading what the ruler of the synagogue said about Jesus healing on the Sabbath day: "There are six days when men ought to work." Then, McPherson changed her voice to characterize Jesus' reply, much to the delight of the audience ("Divine Healing").

Elsewhere McPherson mimicked the sassy tone of an infidel who reasoned, "Well, I don't believe that the Lord Jesus Christ . . . can wash away my sins." In answer to the infidel she narrated how a preacher responded calmly and matter-of-factly, "Well, you and Paul are quite agreed on that subject." Puzzled, the infidel asked, "How? Does Paul agree with me that the blood of Jesus cannot wash away my sins?" "Yes," said the preacher, "turn to the first chapter of Corinthians and the sixteenth verse, and you'll read, 'For the preaching of the cross is to them that perish foolishness but unto us that are saved it is the power of God' " ("Life Begins at Foursquare"). Ebeling argues that the rhetorical technique of dialogue "added the realistic give-and-take of conversation as stimuli to the imagination of her listeners" (157). Without the use of mimicry and dialogue, it is doubtful that McPherson would have been as successful as she was.

Histrionics were a way of life for McPherson. She would frequently march across the stage gesturing "with her whole body, her right hand jabbing the air and then reaching out to touch the audience" (Austin 3). Not only did she preach, but she also sang, cried, and prayed in front of her followers. During her illustrated sermon "Big Bad Wolf," for example, "Sister" sang, "Who's afraid of the big bad wolf, the big bad wolf, the big bad wolf; Who's afraid of the big bad wolf, tra la la la la." According to Austin, some believed that Mc-

Pherson put on "the best show in town." This was no small feat given the fact that she was performing in Hollywood where entertainment and movie stars were not in short supply.

McPherson knew she was dramatic, and proud of it. Once she stated, "I know people who say, 'My, you should see sister McPherson. She talks too loud and she waves her arms.' Well . . . they'd like to turn me into a pillar of salt." Not pleased with this fate, McPherson continued, "Wouldn't I look grand up here preaching. . . . And I'd be talking to a whole lot of empty seats. I'm glad I am alive." She despised what she termed "applejohn" preachers, those who were boring and "dried up" ("Divine Healing").

After her visit to a McPherson revival, Comstock noted how McPherson possessed a nervous mannerism. She wrote how "Sister's" hands "tell the tale of nervous tension." The rest of her body "appears completely relaxed." "Her chest is full with big breathing, her movements are swingingly free. But watch her hands while others are performing [in the illustrated sermon]; they play restlessly, interlacing, touching a lock of hair, adjusting a cuff, collar, wrist-watch. They never relax except as she forces them to do so" (18). Despite this quirk in her delivery, it in no way appeared to negatively impact her listeners' ability to stay focused on the sermon.

CONCLUSION

Like other faith healers that will be covered in subsequent chapters, McPherson believed that the devil was the cause of sickness and disease. To her, he was still "the accuser of the brethren" (*Divine Healing Sermons* 82). And while McPherson believed in doctors, she also believed there came a time when doctors could do no more (91). God, however, could heal whatever the ailment.

In an attempt to convince her blue-collar, fundamentalist audiences that miraculous cures were normative for the twentieth century, "Sister" relied on a wide array of rhetorical proofs to meet their needs and expectations. These included frequent appeals to scripture and generous doses of primary and secondary testimonies, as well as appeals to her longevity in the faith healing business. All of these, of course, were attractively packaged in a narrative style of humility and compassion. Her charismatic, yet sensual stage presence also contributed to her fascination. Her dynamism was helped in part from a strong, high-pitched voice that was used in mimicry and dialogue.

There were other prominent faith healers in the early part of this century—men such as Alexander Dowie, Charles Price, and the British Smith Wigglesworth—but none would rise to the level of popularity that "Sister" did. She, perhaps more so than anyone prior to World War II, captured the essence of what it meant to be a healing revivalist. Everywhere she went, thousands collapsed upon her as if drawn by some magnetic force. It was all to end tragically, however, in an Oakland hotel in September 1944 much to the anguish of thousands of her followers. With perhaps the exception of Oral Roberts, who would emerge on the scene four years after McPherson's death and one year prior to the start of evangelist Billy Graham, the twentieth century has not known a healing evangelist as popular as Aimee Semple McPherson. Due to extraordinary rhetorical abilities, her run was nothing short of phenomenal.

REFERENCES

Austin, Alvyn. *Aimee Semple McPherson*. Dan Mills, Ontario: Fitzhenry and Whiteside Limited, 1980.

Bahr, Robert. *Least of All Saints: The Story of Aimee Semple McPherson*. Englewood Cliffs, NJ: Prentice-Hall, Inc., 1979.

Bartow, Charles L. "Just Now: Aimee Semple McPherson's Performance and Preaching of Jesus." *The Journal of Communication and Religion* 20.1 (April 1997): 71–79.

Bissell, Shelton. "Vaudeville at Angelus Temple." *The Outlook* 23 May 1928: 126–27, 158.

Blumhofer, Edith L. *Aimee Semple McPherson: Everybody's Sister*. Grand Rapids, MI: William B. Eerdmans Publishing Co., 1993.

Budlong, Judith N. "Aimee Semple McPherson." *The Nation* 19 June 1929: 737–39.

Butler, Jon. "The Faith of Narrative." *The Yale Review* 82.3 (July 1994): 139–45.

Comstock, Sarah. "Aimee Semple McPherson: Prima Donna of Revivalism." *Harper's Magazine* Dec. 1927: 11–19.

Ebeling, Harry. "Aimee S. McPherson: Evangelist of the City." *Western Speech* 21 (Summer, 1957): 153–59.

Epstein, Daniel Mark. *Sister Aimee: The Life of Aimee Semple McPherson*. New York: Harcourt Brace Jovanovich, 1993.

Fisher, Walter R. "Narration As a Human Communication Paradigm: The Case of Public Moral Argument." *Communication Monographs* 51 (1984): 1–22.

Hadden, Jeffrey K., and Charles E. Swann. *Prime Time Preachers*. Reading, MA: Addison-Wesley, 1981.

Harrell, David Edwin. *All Things Are Possible: The Healing and Charismatic Revivals in Modern America*. Bloomington, IN: Indiana University Press, 1975.

Lewis, Todd V. "Charismatic Communication and Faith Healers: A Critical Study of Rhetorical Behavior." Diss. Louisiana State University, 1980.

McLoughlin, William G. "Aimee Semple McPherson: 'Your Sister in the King's Glad Service.' " *The Journal of Popular Culture* 1 (Winter, 1967): 193–217.

McPherson, Aimee Semple. "Big Bad Wolf." Radio Sermon, n.d.

———. "Divine Healing." Radio Sermon, n.d.

———. *Divine Healing Sermons*. Los Angeles: Biola Press, 1921.

———. "From Milkpail to Pulpit: Life Story of Aimee Semple McPherson." Videocassette. Dir. Pam Gordon. R.P.G. Film and Video, Inc., n.d.

———. "Heaven Can Wait." Radio Sermon, n.d.

———. *In the Service of the King: The Story of My Life*. New York: Boni and Liveright, 1927.

———. "Life Begins at Foursquare." Radio Sermon, n.d.

———. "Livewire." Radio Sermon, n.d.

———. "Many Members, One Body." Radio Sermon, n.d.

———. "Milkpail to Pulpit." Radio Sermon, n.d.

———. "Power of Faith." Radio Sermon, n.d.

———. "Seven Keys to Power." Radio Sermon, n.d.

———. "Seven Sneezes of Shunnen." Radio Sermon, n.d.

———. "Tale of Two Cities." Radio Sermon, n.d.

———. "This is My Task." Radio Sermon, n.d.

———. *This is That*. New York: Garland Publishing, Inc., 1985.

———. "The Zero Hour." Radio Sermon, n.d.

McPherson, Rolf K. "There She Built an Altar." Radio Sermon, n.d.

McWilliams, Carey. "Aimee Semple McPherson: 'Sunlight in My Soul.' " *The Aspirin Age: 1919–1941*. Ed. Isabel Leighton. New York: Simon and Schuster, 1976. 50–80.

Reynolds, Quentin. "Vanishing Evangelist." *Saturday Review* 23 May 1959: 35–36.

Schuetz, Janice. "Storytelling and Preaching: A Case Study of Aimee Semple McPherson." *Religious Communication Today* 9 (Sept. 1986): 29–36.

"Sister Aimee." *Los Angeles History Project*. Narr. Gena Rowlands. Prod. Kathleen Dowdey and Jan Dannenbaum. KCET-TV, Los Angeles, 1990.

Thomas, Lately. *Storming Heaven: The Lives and Turmoils of Minnie Kennedy and Aimee Semple McPherson.* New York: William Morrow and Co., 1970.

Time. 9 Oct. 1944: 58, 60.

Weaver, Richard M. *Language Is Sermonic: Richard M. Weaver on the Nature of Language.* Ed. Richard L. Johannesen, Rennard Strickland, and Ralph T. Eubanks. Baton Rouge: Louisiana State University Press, 1970.

Worthington, William. "Healing at Angelus Temple." *The Christian Century.* (24 April 1929): 549–52.

CHAPTER TWO

From "Sassafras Country Boy" to World-Renown Preacher: Revivalist William Branham

In his book *All Things Are Possible* historian David E. Harrell suggests that with the passing of pioneer healing evangelists Charles Price, Smith Wigglesworth, and Aimee Semple McPherson in the 1940s, Pentecostalism experienced a void. While old Pentecostals fondly reminisced about a former time when miracles were commonplace, young Pentecostals who had never witnessed them yearned for the same experience. Indeed, old Pentecostals worried that the days of miracles had ended as young Pentecostals hungered for a revival of their own (18–20). Such concern, however, was short-lived.

Although he had been preaching as a Baptist minister since 1933, in 1946 a man by the name of William Marrion Branham burst onto the healing-revival scene. Well into the next decade, he and men like Oral Roberts, A. A. Allen, and Jack Coe, to name a few, would fill the positions vacated by their healing predecessors. For the time being, at least, the day had been saved.

Looked upon by historians as the "initiator," "pacesetter," and "most revered leader" of the healing revival that erupted in the late 1940s, William Branham was enormously popular and influential (Harrell 25; Weaver 58). During his meetings thousands flocked into tents and auditoriums to hear him preach, receive their miracle, or

William Branham's famous "halo" picture taken January 24, 1950 in Houston. Courtesy of Billy Graham Center Archives, Wheaton College, Wheaton, Illinois. Reprinted with permission of Pearry Green, minister of The Tucson Tabernacle and personal friend of William Branham.

merely watch as Branham administered "healing" to the physically and emotionally afflicted. Gordon Lindsey, one of Branham's managers, reports that in one of his earliest meetings in Jonesboro, Arkansas, "People had gathered . . . from twenty-eight states and Mexico, and some 25,000 . . . attended the meeting." Since no hotel accommodations were available within a fifty-mile radius, individuals were forced to live in tents, trailers, and trucks while others slept in their cars (93). Lindsey also reports that in another one-night meeting early in Branham's career, some 12,000 people packed into Kiel Auditorium in St. Louis to hear him preach and watch him administer healings (91). In a meeting in Louisville in 1950 Branham reported his audience to be between 7,000 to 10,000 strong and informed those in attendance that they were the smallest second-night crowd "since I've been in the field" (T1 1950). In perhaps one of his most famous services in Houston, January 1950, Branham attracted a crowd of 8,000 in a single service (Lindsey 151; see also Weaver 50). Such figures testify to Branham's success as a healing revivalist.

Not only were the crowds large, but so were the healing lines that formed, especially during Branham's early meetings. Branham disclosed that once in Phoenix he prayed for 2,500 people in one afternoon to receive healing or salvation. "That's the longest prayer line I ever had," recalled Branham, "Twenty-five hundred people one afternoon, approximately that many, maybe a little more, a little less" (T410). Branham confessed that because he could not continue to minister to such large crowds each night he was forced to adopt the practice of having individuals—randomly selected—to fill out prayer cards, which numbered from one to one hundred. Sometimes, he gave out as little as fifty. Usually either Branham or one of his managers would explain to the audience how prayer cards worked and why such a limited number were distributed prior to a healing service (T1).

In time Branham would develop an international reputation. After having held revivals and healing services in the United States from 1946 through 1950—with the exception of a six-month hiatus in 1948 in which he resigned due to "nervous exhaustion"—Branham began a tour of Europe (Harrell 32–33; Weaver 49). In April 1950 he held his first European meetings in Finland and Norway where more than 7,000 persons attended nightly services. In 1952 he visited South Africa where some 30,000 answered the altar call at Durban alone. Weaver points out that it was Branham's success in South Africa that prompted the writing of Julius Stadsklev's book *William Branham: A*

Prophet Visits South Africa. In 1954 Branham returned to Europe, preaching in Portugal and Rome. That same year he preached in India. By 1954 estimates suggested that he had converted over one-half million people. In 1955 he held meetings in Switzerland and Germany. These were to be his final major revivals overseas (Weaver 51–52).

Problems arose in 1955. Branham's popularity began to wane significantly due to his financial problems and dogmatic teachings. Harrell chronicles how the unsophisticated Branham was incapable of matching wits with selfish managers who took advantage of him financially. To compound the problem the Internal Revenue Service sued him in 1956 for tax evasion (Harrell 39). Moreover, Branham began to preach a rigid code of morality, railing against such foibles as "bobbed hair" and women in "slacks." Other problems with Branham's teachings included his anti-denominational stand, his preaching on oneness, his views on predestination, and his 1963 revelation that he was "the seventh angel" mentioned in Revelation 10:7. Such views served merely to alienate Branham from organized Pentecostal groups. Tragically in 1965 Branham died on Christmas Eve in Amarillo, Texas as the result of injuries sustained in a car wreck on December 18 (Harrell 163–64). Pentecostalism had lost one of its most popular and influential, if not controversial figures who, in the words of Weaver, "had reignited a significant movement in religious America that remains on the scene today" (58).

Although Branham's popularity and influence dropped off dramatically beginning around 1955, for at least nine years he rode the crest of success. No healing revivalist, including Oral Roberts, was more sought after than Branham. Given the fact that he was so influential in taking the Pentecostal message of healing to thousands, perhaps millions, during a nine-year period, the obvious question is, "Why?" What was it about Branham's rhetoric that endeared him to so many people? How was it that Branham was able to induce symbolically so many people to believe that they could be miraculously healed?

While over 1200 sermons exist either in audio, video, or print form, it takes little exposure to Branham's material to deduce his conscious or unconscious rhetorical strategies, especially since he repeats himself so much across so many sermons as I will attempt to demonstrate. Furthermore, as was common with many preachers in this study, Branham preached many of the same sermons over and over again in different cities.

Some scholarly material has already been written about Branham from a historical perspective that addresses reasons for his success. Harrell, for example, was the first to suggest that much of Branham's success was due to his "humility and simplicity" (162). In the most definitive work on Branham, Weaver includes a discussion of several non-rhetorical factors for Branham's success. In addition to agreeing with Harrell about Branham's humility, Weaver cites the "effective leadership" of Branham's managers, skillful publicity, ecumenical preaching, which avoided doctrinal conflict among Pentecostals, and "magnetism of his healing gift" (52–56). Furthermore, Weaver spends an entire chapter focusing on Branham's theology and methodology of healing (59–89). Despite these excellent sources, more could be said in addressing Branham's popularity and *modus operandi*, particularly from a rhetorical perspective.

BRANHAM'S FOLLOWERS

Before elucidating Branham's rhetorical appeals, it is important to understand who his audience was, or at least to understand who Branham perceived them to be. One of the earliest external references to Branham's followers is found in the July 14, 1947, issue of *Time* magazine, which reported that in one of Branham's services, the "little farm town of Vandalia, Ill. just about doubled its population in one day. Some 4,000 newcomers, almost all of them blind, deaf, lame or incurably ill, were there to be healed" (20). Judging by the number of cots on and around the podium in a picture of the Ice Arena in Tacoma, Washington May 12–17, 1948, one realizes that many who sought Branham appeared to be severely afflicted. Moreover, these images square neatly with the types of people who sought out Branham as described in Lindsey's book *William Branham: A Man Sent from God*. Lindsey, for example, mentions several cases of deaf, dumb, and blind people coming to Branham's meetings and begging for his help.

Even Branham himself recognized those who attended his meetings were different from the audiences of other non-Pentecostal evangelists of his day. Once, for example, he related the story of hearing "a fine brother" preach to a group of about 1,800 "nice, well-dressed people, intelligent-looking people," all of whom were non-Pentecostal. Juxtaposing his own audience to that of the non-Pentecostal preacher's, Branham recalled, "I thought, 'My that's very nice.' But here come [sic] my group in. Mine come [sic] in on crutches, wheelchairs, [and] straight jackets" (T410).

The above quote clearly suggests that Branham believed those who attended his meetings were qualitatively different than those who attended revivals of mainline ministers—economically, educationally, and physically. Certainly not everyone in Branham's audiences were socially or physically handicapped, but thousands sought him out during his lifetime to receive something they did not possess— deliverance from their diseases. The kinds of people who flocked to Branham's meetings are generally found in the campaigns of faith healers (see Pullum, "Sisters" 115–16). This is not surprising because often preachers like Branham provide the only hope for the physically and mentally incurable. Hoffer notes, "People whose lives are barren and insecure seem to show a greater willingness to obey than people who are self-sufficient and self-confident" (115). This much was clear to Branham who geared his message to meet the needs of these individuals. Branham provided hope for the hopeless, much like other faith healers before and after him (Pullum, "Sisters"; see also Pullum, "Ernest Angley"). Branham believed that God can heal even after "a lovely doctor had done all that he can do" (T56).

BRANHAM'S ABILITY TO APPEAL TO COMMON PEOPLE

Branham was revered by so many followers in part because he had the ability to appeal to the common man or woman. In an often quoted passage from his *Rhetoric of Motives* Burke writes, "you persuade a man only insofar as you can talk his language by speech, gesture, tonality, order, image, attitude, idea, identifying your ways with his" (55). Burke believed that an individual persuaded another person when he or she "identified" with or became "consubstantial" with that person. There were a number of ways Branham bridged whatever gap there may have been between an internationally famous healing revivalist and ordinary, "everyday" people.

One way Branham achieved identification with those who sought him was through his humility and sincerity. Although both Harrell (162) and Weaver (55) have already made this point, it bears repeating here with specific illustrations from Branham's discourse. Sounding like the female faith healers Aimee Semple McPherson, Kathryn Kuhlman, and Gloria Copeland (Pullum, "Sisters"), Branham was always quick to give God the credit for healings that occurred in his assemblies. Once, for example, Branham reminded his audience, "I do not claim to do one thing myself. I have no power within myself to do anything" (T56). Elsewhere he clarified, "No one can heal you except God. He's the only one that can help you" (T50A). During a meeting in 1952 Branham prayed, as he often did, "Lord, sanctify thy servant just now . . . and I pray, Father, . . . that you'll let your great, glorious power be known to everyone and if thy unworthy servant has found grace in thy sight for tonight, may you take this unworthy person, move the being out and come in" (V1). Branham's personal manager Gordon Lindsey believed that it was Branham's "simple humility that has charmed his audiences wherever he has been" (11). One would be hard pressed to disagree with Lindsey's assessment. Branham would never dream of placing himself above his audience. Even though he claimed to be a seer—one sent from God himself—he still maintained, "that's not make [sic] me any more than that drunkard that was converted ten minutes ago somewhere. . . . He is a Christian the same as I am. . . . There's no great people and big people in the kingdom of God. We're all one" (T246).

Alan Monroe, a contemporary rhetorical theorist of Branham's day, suggests that "many a speech awkwardly given has been made eloquent by the . . . sincerity of the speaker" (15). Monroe went on to say, "Straight-forward sincerity is the best assurance of effective speaking" (56). Although Branham probably never read Monroe, he certainly personified Monroe's advice. In spite of whatever shortcomings in speech training Branham might have suffered—and they were numerous—he more than made up for them through his humble and sincere attitudes. Such attitudes allowed him to achieve consubstantiation with a mass of people who had no reason to be anything other than humble since their situations in life forced them into humility in the first place.

Not only did his humility appear in his disavowing of personal miraculous powers, but Branham never claimed to be a well educated or effective speaker, another way in which he achieved identification with his audiences. In fact he disclosed once, "I'm a very very poor speaker" (T410). On another occasion he confessed, "I'm not much of a scholar because I never got the . . . education—seventh grade at that" (T74). Elsewhere he divulged, "I'm just a man—unlearned, uneducated" (T56). At one point, sounding as if he were relieved not to be well educated, Branham claimed, "Education . . . has been the greatest curse Christianity has ever had" (T410). Such statements served to create a bond between him and the ordinary, uneducated members of his audiences.

If, as Burke suggests, a speaker persuades another person "insofar as you can talk his language by speech, gesture, tonality," etc., certainly Branham's nonstandard grammar and heavy rural accent helped him persuade his uneducated followers (55). Weaver correctly notes that Branham's speech was "replete with grammatical errors" (55). One needs to listen only to a sermon or two before this much is evident. Once, for instance, in telling how long prayer lines in one city were, Branham remarked, "Prayer lines was [sic] way down the street" (T1). In another sermon he said, "It is true that many people doesn't [sic] dream" (V1). Once he prayed to God, "I have did [sic] this all at thy command." Subject-verb agreement and correct verb tense were certainly not Branham's forte.

Not only did Branham frequently employ the wrong verb, but on occasion, he had problems with his pronunciation. For example, instead of correctly pronouncing the disease "multiple sclerosis," Branham called it "multiple cirrhosis" (T1). On another occasion, "Arkansas" became "Are Kansas" (T56) and "yesterday" became "yesterdee" (T1). Numerous other examples could be cited but these are sufficient to show that Branham was an unpolished speaker who identified with an unpolished audience through nonstandard speech and mispronunciation of words. His business manager Gordon Lindsey once wrote of him, "The clear, simple style of Rev. Branham possesses its own charm and though he himself boasts no cultural advantages, this style, though at times rugged . . . has a distinction of its own" (9–10).

Indeed Branham's speech was charming to most of those who listened to him. His poor grammar and mispronunciation simply did not seem to matter to him. For Branham and his listeners there were more important things with which to be concerned. Still, one wonders to what extent Branham was conscious of his poor grammar, mispronunciation, and heavy rural accent as rhetorical assets.

A final way Branham achieved identification with his audience was through the contents of his storytelling. Like other faith healers (see Pullum, "Sisters" and "Angley"), Branham related narratives about how poor he was while growing up. Calling himself a "sassafras country boy" (Footprints 31), Branham confessed, "we was [sic] very poor, just the poorest of poor" (Footprints 20). Occasionally he told his life story about being born in a dirt-floor log cabin near Berksville, Kentucky. He related how, as a boy, he would go to town on Saturday nights with his family in a mule-drawn wagon to buy coal oil and peppermint candy. He told stories about his father's shaving brush made out of corn "shuck" and how much he enjoyed eating the crust of pan-baked corn bread with beans and "hog jowl." Branham narrated that when married he and his first wife Hope rented a two-room house while he earned only twenty cents a day. They began their married lives together with an old stove purchased for $1.75 and an unpainted table from Sears and Roebuck (T118A). During his career, much to the delight of his audiences, Branham boasted, "I'd rather be poor and live in a shack and have favor with God" than have "all the wealth the world owns" (T56). Branham taught that "the best of hearts . . . beat under overalls." Furthermore, he had little use for "put ons." Delighting his listeners he disclosed, "I like real old fashion men and women" (T1).

Relating stories of humble beginnings merely served to tighten the bond between Branham and his followers. Since they, too, probably had little money or status in life, they could identify with one like themselves. Moreover, although Branham took money from his followers to support his ministry, he was careful never to let them forget that even though he was a popular and influential minister, he was not in business to become rich and famous. "I'm not here tonight to be seen or heard," suggested Branham in one of his sermons. "I'm not here because of finance. You know that, so I'm here for one thing—because I love Jesus and I love you" (V1). Once Branham contended, "I never took an offering in my life" from the "little Baptist Church" in Jeffersonville, Indiana where he began his ministry. He related how he worked for many years as a game warden which allowed him to preach (T50A). Such statements convinced his constituency that he had loftier goals than making money and becoming popular.

BRANHAM'S ABILITY TO EVOKE EMOTIONS THROUGH STORYTELLING

Not only was the content of Branham's stories rhetorically powerful in that they created common ground between him and his audience, but the *manner* in which he related them was equally impressive. When telling his life story, Branham relied heavily on the

Aristotelian notion of pathos. In other words, Branham appealed to the emotions of his audience. Not only could he bring an audience to tears but he could also cause them to laugh hysterically.

In what may be one of the saddest personal stories ever told by a public speaker, Branham related the loss of his first wife Hope and his infant daughter Sharon during the Ohio River flood of 1937 near Jeffersonville, Indiana. Branham cried aloud as he related how he lost his father, brother, wife, and "baby girl" all within six months of each other. Sobbing as he told of kneeling by the bedside of his dying wife, he related how she rallied from death long enough to ask him why he called her back from going to Jesus. Branham related how she asked him to promise her to find a good, Holy Ghost-filled woman to marry and to buy a new rifle that they weren't able to afford while they were married. In loud and dramatic fashion, Branham went on to tell about how, while kneeling beside the bed of his infant daughter Sharon, whose "little leg" was jerking from meningitis, he yelled out to the Lord, "Heavenly Father, please don't take her." Branham promised God that he would never look down on Pentecostals again if God would spare her. Branham sadly related how after Sharon's death he became depressed to the point of putting a gun to his head and contemplating suicide before he fell asleep and dreamed about a woman with blonde hair in heaven who called him "Dad." In emotional fashion, Branham related how he was in heaven talking with his daughter Sharon and wife Hope (T118B).

On another occasion, in graphic, heart-wrenching fashion, Branham reiterated how he lost his father and brother along with his wife and daughter:

> I laid my daddy on my arm, saw his hair drop down, and he looked at me—he went to meet God. I saw my brother yonder struggling, the veins cut, and his neck broke, and the blood flying from his mouth. And I looked at my wife and she said, 'I'll meet you just across the border yonder, Billy.'
>
> I laid my hand on my baby the next day, seeing it's little leg jerking. I said, 'Bless your little heart, Sharon. Daddy will meet you on the other side' ("The Inner Veil" 35).

Rhetorical theorist Alan Monroe points out that the "normal condition" of an audience is one of "mental inertia" and "emotional equilibrium" unless the speaker stirs them through some type of appeal. He argues that if the speaker is to accomplish what he or she purposes, then he or she must overcome this inertia or "counteract an opposite tendency" by puncturing an audience's apathy, which will, in turn, "make them feel unsatisfied until they have reacted as you wish" (194). One way to remove apathy, suggests Monroe, is to evoke the emotion of sympathy or pity. "To do so," he instructs, "remember that you must make it easy for them to identify themselves with the unfortunate ones, to put themselves in the other's shoes. This you cannot accomplish with statistics and abstractions; you must describe individuals and describe them vividly" (205–6). If this be the case, certainly Branham was able to persuade his audiences through the vivid stories he told about his relatives. Not only was the content often heart-wrenching, but the dramatic manner in which he told them would have caused his listeners to sympathize with him. It is hard to imagine how anyone could listen to Branham and not feel the pain that he himself felt during the loss of his relatives. Only the most calloused of listeners could not be moved emotionally upon hearing Branham narrate such tales of woe.

In addition to his somber side, Branham had an excellent sense of humor. For instance, Branham told of how one warm spring day he wore an old coat to school to hide the fact that he had no shirt to wear. Branham humorously told of how his teacher tried to persuade him to take off his coat. During the same sermon he comically told of how he asked his wife to marry him in a letter because he did not have the nerve to ask her in person. He related how he and his wife walked to church together one Wednesday evening and how he wondered all the way to church and back whether she received the letter and what her reaction to it might have been. Throughout both of these narratives, Branham's audience laughed hard and often (T118A). Clearly, Branham could be very humorous if the occasion called for it. Like other faith healers, Branham was entertaining to watch (Pullum "Sisters").

James Winans, another contemporary rhetorical theorist of Branham, suggests that "an audience will listen as long as it is amused, and that a good laugh may banish weariness and hostility" (155). Winans argues that one way a speaker can employ humor is through an amusing anecdote or story. In spite of this, warns Winans, a speaker should not "keep an audience 'convulsed with laughter' all the time. It is better 'to mix grave and gay.' " Branham was a master

at this. Although he told humorous stories, he always came around
to a serious point. Usually Branham articulated how God would eventually see him through whatever hardship or disaster in life he suffered.

BRANHAM'S USE OF EXAMPLES AND TESTIMONIES

Like all faith healers (see Pullum "Sisters" and "Angley"), Branham
relied heavily on personal experiences and testimonies to induce his
audiences to believe that they could receive a personal healing. While
onlookers frequently witnessed Branham heal people on stage and in
the audience from diseases like throat goiters, breast cancer, gall-
bladder ailments, "ruptures," headaches, and so forth, more often
than not Branham would testify of healings he had personally witnessed (V1). Once, for example, he boasted that he had "never seen
any cross-eyed child ever come to the platform but what was healed.
And we've seen better than three hundred cases of cross-eyeds healed
in less than six months time." In the same sermon, he testified of a
man being healed who "had been paralyzed for ten years." He told
stories about an eighteen-year-old boy with a withered hand, a little
girl with braces, a crippled man who had been thrown from a horse,
and a woman possessed with a demon having been healed (T1). Branham testified that he had seen blind people healed in his services "and
less than five minutes" later they were reading their Bibles (T50B).
Branham boasted of seeing miracles such as those above "hundreds
of times" in his lifetime (T1).

Not only did Branham talk about healings he had seen, but, like
other faith healers (see Pullum, "Sisters" and "Angley") he testified
to having received a healing himself. After a Baptist preacher anointed
him with oil and prayed for him, he was healed of "stomach trouble."
After his healing, reported Branham, "I went right down home and
we had cornbread, beans, and onions for dinner" (Footprints 96).

In short Branham made sure that his audiences understood that
"every person [who] comes to this platform is healed. There's been
nothing no matter how bad it's been twisted, crippled, or afflicted. It
always healed. . . . There's been some hideous cases" (T1). In citing
such examples, Branham was unwittingly following Monroe's advice
to "avoid generalities and abstractions" in persuasion. "Incidents
which are recent, which have occurred frequently, or which were in-

tensely important at the time they happened are the most powerful material with which to build up the speech for conviction. No other single factor is so important in this type of speech as presenting facts, pertinent facts—and then more facts!" (442).

If an audience were ever skeptical of Branham's "facts," he tried to remove all doubt by evoking the credibility of a third party. Once he asked a Reverend Hooper who was sitting in the back of the building to verify his story of a woman who had been released by demons and immediately told his audience to write "Reverend Mr. G. H. Brown" who lived at "505 Victory Street" in Little Rock, Arkansas if they needed further proof. Regarding the man who was thrown from a horse, Branham told his listeners that "Brother Bosworth" examined the man and verified his healing. Branham disclosed that he had 40,000 testimonies of healed people signed by doctors. On one occasion he even invoked the credibility of the *Chicago Tribune* newspaper. Upon showing a report from the *Chicago Tribune* about nine deaf, dumb, and blind youths who had been healed at one of Branham's meetings, Branham boasted, "Newspapers like *Chicago Tribune* are not fanatics." "Them cases have to be absolutely thoroughly examined before they can be placed in a paper like that" (T1). Such references to third party sources reinforced Branham's personal claims of healings he had witnessed. Or, as Monroe suggests, "Frequently an audience which will not take your word alone will be convinced or impressed by the statement of someone else" (232). Branham certainly understood this and used testimony to his benefit.

BRANHAM'S RHETORICAL REFERENCES TO THE BIBLE

If personal examples and third-party claims were not enough to persuade his followers to believe in miracles, then Branham's invoking of the scriptures would help. Using the Bible to prove miracles was an effective strategy for Branham because his Pentecostal followers already held it in such high esteem, believing that its stories and references to miraculous healing were normative for the people of the twentieth century. Winans argues that one of the many ways a speaker can persuade an audience is to find "a common ground of belief." "Good feeling," argues Winans, "results when the audience sees that the speaker's views are in some respects in harmony with their own; and this tends to the belief that his present proposal is not, after all, impossible" (337). Since Branham's Pentecostal audiences already believed the Bible, all Branham had to do was merely reference it without going into some convoluted discussion about why the passages supported his life's work. In fact that is all Branham ever did. In relating the story of his own healing from "stomach trouble" Branham poetically recalled, "every promise in the Book is mine, every chapter, every verse, every line; . . . I am trusting in His Word Divine, for every promise in the Book is mine" (Footprints 96).

Branham often read from the gospels where Jesus healed people. One of his favorite stories involved Christ's healing the man lying by the pool of Bethesda as found in John 5 (T56 and V2). Additionally, Branham referenced passages such as Psalms 103:1–3, which says in part, "Bless the Lord . . . who healeth all thy diseases" (T1). Another favorite passage of Branham and used often by other faith healers (see Pullum "Sisters" and "Angley") was Isaiah 53:5 and I Peter 2:24, which state in part, "He was wounded for our transgressions and with His stripes we are healed" (T56). Branham was also fond of Mark 16:17–18 to prove that the miracles he performed were a sign from God: "And these signs shall follow them that believe. . . . they shall lay hands on the sick and they shall recover" (T63). After reading Exodus 23:20-ff, Branham argued that God will provide signs and wonders in his day "for the faith of the people" just as he did in Moses's day (T50A). Branham's favorite Biblical phrase, however, was the fact that "Jesus Christ is the same yesterday, today, and forever" ("God Called Man" 4; "God's Eagles" 429; and T1). He believed "there never was nothing that come [sic] before Jesus Christ . . . but what he was more than a match for. And he's just the same today as he was yesterday and will be forever. And he proves that and you'll see that night after night." Branham argued that if this were not the case, "you'll have a right to doubt him" (T1).

Knowing that his audience already believed in divine healing because they believed the above passages proved it, Branham argued, albeit illogically, "The very reason that you believe in divine healing proves there is a divine healing" (V1). Moreover, he tried to place his audiences into a mind set to see miraculous healings while simultaneously preempting any criticism by stating, "You get what you expect." He then confidently avowed, "I'm expecting tonight to see the Holy Spirit come and manifest himself in power" (V1).

BRANHAM'S VISIONS, ANGELIC VISITATIONS, AND SIGNS FROM GOD

Perhaps one of Branham's most persuasive strategies to convince his followers that they could be healed and that he was God's agent to bring it about involved his disclosure of visions and visitations by angels. In fact Branham told such stories hundreds of times throughout his career. One of his earliest and most well-known visitations occurred when he was only seven years old, when an angel said to him, "Don't drink or smoke or defile your body in any way, there'll be a work for you to do when you get older" (T50A; T118A; Footprints 60).

Another very popular visitation occurred on May 7, 1946, when Branham was thirty-seven. Branham recounts how in the early hours of the morning he was praying in a room when he saw a pillar of fire and a two hundred pound man with shoulder-length dark hair and bare feet appear to him (V2). The angel, as Branham described him, said "in a real deep voice," "Do not fear, I am sent from the Presence of the Almighty God." Branham said that he recognized the voice— the same voice that spoke to him when he was only seven years old. The angel went on to say, "Your peculiar birth and misunderstood life has been to indicate that you're to go to all the world and pray for the sick people." The angel continued, "If you get the people to believe you, and be sincere when you pray, nothing shall stand before your prayers, not even cancer" (Footprints 74; Lindsey 77). Branham believed that this was his official commissioning by the Lord.

Branham often reminded his audiences of two signs the angel gave to him as proof, just as God had given Moses signs "to a-vindicate his ministry." The first sign, according to the angel, was for Branham to feel "a physical effect that'll happen on your body" when Branham would grasp an individual's right hand with his left. "Then you pray. And if it leaves, the disease is gone from the people. If it doesn't leave, just ask a blessing and walk away" (Footprints 75; T50B).

Perhaps as a conscious rhetorical strategy, Branham would often remove his watch prior to receiving people in his prayer lines because, as he claimed, the vibrations from his hand would "stop that watch dead still," which was why his Longines watch was "in the shop" (T50A; T1). Additionally, Branham disclosed that often his hand would be "so numb" after a healing service that he would "have to run hot water over it for near half hour to get feelings back to it again" (T1). These types of comments became further proof to his audiences that he had been sent from God to minister to the sick.

A second sign given to Branham was the ability to discern people's hearts. "This they will hear," assured the angel who spoke to Branham (Footprints 75). During his meetings Branham often reminded people who would come on stage to be healed that he had never met nor seen them before. He would then proceed to tell them why they were there, leaving the audience with the impression that he had discerned their conditions. He would discern people's diseases, ranging from anemia to heart trouble to cancer, to name a few. After reminding one woman that she and he were strangers, Branham proceeded to explain that someone had told a lie on her, that a man had called her a "witch," and that her whole church was "stirred up" over it. And, to make matters worse, her pastor had polio. After Branham admonished, "Sister, don't pay no attention [to] what them people tell you. . . . They're a lyin'," the audience erupted in applause (V2; "God's Eagles"). If there had been any skepticism in the minds of the audience that Branham had been commissioned by God, this instance—and hundreds of others like it during his ministry—would have removed any doubt, for he left the audience with the impression that he had been told this information from a supernatural source. These kinds of events were powerful rhetorical illustrations to the "true believers" in attendance.

BRANHAM'S PREEMPTION OF SKEPTICISM

A master at persuading people, Branham had a way of preempting criticism. Occasionally he dealt with those who believed that what he did was mere "psychology." Confessing that there was some psychology involved, Branham argued, "If what I do is psychology then Paul used it" when he told a man, "I perceive you have faith to be healed. Stand up on your feet." Branham explained, "It's the mind of Christ in the Christian moving" (T50B). Here Branham identified what he did with what an apostle of God had done on another occasion. If healings were in any way related to psychology, Branham was willing to accept this fact as long as the apostles themselves had engaged in it. Branham's audiences were not willing to accept the apostles' healings as mere psychology, though. Neither, then, would they be likely to attribute what Branham did to psychology alone.

Branham also had an answer for those who were skeptical as to why individuals were never healed despite the fact that they had been through a healing line. Branham pointed out that healing lasts only as long as faith lasts. He likened healing to a person who comes to Christ one day but "tomorrow can be a child of the devil." "It's when he loses faith in God what sends him back," Branham rustically argued (T1). He taught that a tumor, for example, which was on the inside of a body, would not drop off on stage for everyone to see but would be cured nonetheless. Problems would arise, however, when it would swell up and a person would begin to feel bad even though the person was really healed. This would cause a person to lose his or her faith. Branham believed a person's "unbelief will bring it [tumor] back again" and taught, "it ain't what you feel, it's what you believe" (V1).

In reality Branham created a no-lose situation for himself. If people really became better, Branham's claim that he had been sent from God to heal people was believed. If people were not healed, the problem was theirs, not Branham's, which did no damage to Branham's credibility.

Branham was also quick to remind people that he was not a "divine healer" anyway. Reasoning by analogy, Branham wanted people to know in no uncertain terms that "preaching divine healing doesn't make you a divine healer no more than preaching salvation makes you a divine savior" (T50B). Claiming not to be a divine healer allowed Branham to escape the responsibility for a person's healing. Even though he was the agent through whom God healed, he himself was not to be saddled with the success or failure of another person's physical well-being. This argument became compelling when juxtaposed to the "divine savior" argument. Just as someone other than Branham (i.e., Jesus and the person being saved) was responsible for salvation—even though Branham was the preacher—someone other than Branham was responsible for healings, even though he himself preached healing.

BRANHAM'S WARNINGS TO CRITICS

Another rhetorical strategy that Branham used, albeit unwittingly, was to warn critics in the audience that if they did not keep their heads bowed and maintain a sense of reverence and decorum during the healing services, something terrible would happen to them. Believing that he was bound by law to make such a disclaimer, Branham often warned skeptics that he could not be responsible for anything bad that might happen to them (T50B; T1). Referencing the story in the New Testament where demons left a man and entered into a herd of swine, Branham cautioned, "I am not responsible for any critic in the meeting. These things [diseases and cursings] go from one to the other." Branham then proceeded to tell of a little girl who was healed of epilepsy, but a critic in the audience who did not bow his head came down with mental problems (T1).

While this kind of argument probably annoyed rather than persuaded unbelievers, it most likely had a reinforcing effect upon Branham's followers. Those who believed already were afraid to entertain whatever skepticism they might have felt, thinking that the things of which Branham warned would happen to them. Not to believe in healings, then, would jeopardize their physical and mental well-being.

BRANHAM'S REFERENCES TO PICTURES

A final rhetorical strategy Branham often employed in his healing services was an occasional reference to one picture or another which supposedly captured an angel, a halo, or some other supernatural phenomenon with Branham. To Branham such records were empirical proof that God was with him, and he made sure the audience knew that such pictures were available for analysis.

Perhaps the most famous picture to come out of Branham's meetings occurred during the Houston campaign during January 1950 in which a light above Branham's head was construed by the Branham organization to be a supernatural halo. Harrell suggests this photograph "became perhaps the most famous relic in the history of the revival" (35).

During the Houston meeting, W. E. Best, Pastor of the Houston Tabernacle Baptist Church, debated F. F. Bosworth on the scripturalness and reality of miraculous healings. Best had hired an independent photographer by the name of Ayers to take pictures of the event. All of the pictures turned out to be blank except for one, which showed a light above Branham's head. Amazed at the picture, Mr. Ayers took it to a Mr. George Lacy, Investigator of Questioned Documents, to be analyzed for its authenticity. In an official document dated January 26, 1950, Mr. Lacey reported in part that the negative "was not retouched nor was it a composite or double exposed negative" (see document in Lindsey). Weaver points out that, after hearing of the "supernatural halo" in the picture taken in Houston, Branham later "calmly" reported that similar situations had occurred before in his ministry (50).

Such professional opinion was all Branham needed to further his assertion that he was doing God's work. In one sermon, for example, Branham referenced the Houston photograph and boldly told his audience that he could sell it because Jesus was good enough to appear with him. Instead of guilt by association, Branham was using validation by association. Shortly after Branham's remarks, his manager Gordon Lindsey stepped to the microphone and told that the negative examined by Mr. Lacey "was absolutely positively genuine" (T50B). Branham informed his audience that this picture was not there that night but that they could examine a copy of it the next day. Simply put, Branham used the photograph as a rhetorical symbol to induce belief in his hearers.

In another sermon Branham mentioned "that picture" with an angel standing beside him. He disclosed how one woman told him, "Brother Branham, that picture don't look like you." Branham remarked that any individual would not look the same if he or she had an angel as close to him or her as Branham did in the picture (T74). While such a statement is ostensibly an innocent response to someone's observation, in reality it served as proof to an audience that God had validated Branham's ministry because he sent an angel to stand beside Branham on the platform and to be photographed no less.

CONCLUSION

It seems as if Branham were constantly trying to justify himself and his actions to his audience through one means or another, either consciously or unconsciously. These rhetorical strategies included numerous appeals to his common followers, ability to evoke emotions through interesting and humorous stories, employment of examples, testimonies, and third-party sources, references to the Bible and angelic visitations, preemptive arguments to skeptics, warnings to critics, and allusions to pictures supposedly containing supernatural phenomenon. In a word, one would have to conclude that Branham was successful with the majority of his followers due in large measure to one or more of these strategies sometimes operating alone, sometimes in combination with others. Given the unsophisticated and desperate conditions of his audience, these arguments form the right dynamics to bring about persuasion for thousands of people who sat at Branham's feet. Perhaps such arguments continue to influence today, some thirty years after Branham's death.

With the exceptions of warnings to critics and allusions to pictures containing the supernatural, what Branham did is common for other faith healers of other times. It is likely that these techniques are passed on from one generation to another. However obtained, it is difficult to separate the strategies of Branham from those of McPherson and other figures in this book.

If Branham had lived beyond 1965, it is hard to say how popular he would have been today. For those who followed him in his heyday, such conjecture is irrelevant. Starting in 1946 Branham was the most popular healing revivalist under any tent or in any coliseum. He was to remain such for at least nine more years due in large measure to the techniques he employed. The truth is only Branham really knew to what extent he was aware of such rhetorical strategies. As we shall see in the next chapter, although they were in many ways quite different men, many of Branham's rhetorical tendencies were like those of his contemporary Oral Roberts.

REFERENCES

Branham, William Marrion. *Footprints on the Sands of Time: The Autobiography of William Marrion Branham*. Jeffersonville, IN: Spoken Word Publications, 1976.

———. "God Called Man." Jeffersonville, IN. Oct. 5, 1958. No. 27. In *The Voice of the Prophet: Messages by William Marrion Branham*. Vol. 2B. Tucson, AZ: Tucson Tabernacle Books, n.d.: 565–601.

———. "God's Eagles." Tulsa, OK. April 2, 1960. No. 12. In *The Voice of the Prophet: Messages by William Marrion Branham*. Vol. 2A. Tucson, AZ: Tucson Tabernacle Books, n.d.: 399–411.

———. "The Inner Veil." Jeffersonville, IN. Jan. 1, 1956. No. 14. In *The Voice of the Prophet: Messages by William Marrion Branham*. Vol. 2A. Tucson, AZ: Tucson Tabernacle Books, n.d.: 469–511.

———. (T1). "Explaining the Ministry and Healing." Audiotape. Louisville, KY. 1950.

————. (T50A). "Obey the Voice of the Angel." Audiotape. Minneapolis, MN. July 13, 1949.

————. (T50B). "At Thy Word." Audiotape. Minneapolis, MN. July 14, 1949.

————. (T56). "I Was Not Disobedient to Vision." Audiotape. Zion, IL. 949.

————. (T63). "Healing and What Sickness Is." Audiotape. Cleveland, OH. Aug. 8, 1950.

————. (T74). "Angel and the Commission." Audiotape. Cleveland, OH. Aug. 21, 1950.

————. (T118A & T118B). "Branham's Life Story." Audiotape. Phoenix, AZ. April 15, 1952.

————. (T246). "Unpardonable Sin." Audiotape. Jeffersonville, IN. Oct. 24, 1954.

————. (T410). "Elijah and Elisha." Audiotape. Phoenix, AZ. 1957.

————. (V1). "Deep Calleth unto Deep." Videotape. Washington, D.C. n.d.

————. (V2). "Twentieth-Century Prophet." Videotape. Jeffersonville, IN. n.d.

Burke, Kenneth. *Rhetoric of Motives*. New York: Prentice-Hall, 1950.

Harrell, David Edwin. *All Things Are Possible: The Healing and Charismatic Revivals in Modern America*. Bloomington, IN: Indiana University Press, 1975.

Hoffer, Eric. *The True Believer*. New York: Harper and Row, 1965.

Lindsey, Gordon. *William Branham: A Man Sent from God*. 3rd ed. Jeffersonville, IN: Spoken Word Publications, 1950.

Monroe, Alan H. *Principles and Types of Speech*. 3rd ed. New York: Scott, Foresman and Company, 1949.

Pullum, Stephen J. "His Speech Betrayeth Him: The Healing Rhetoric of Ernest Angley, Akron's Nationally Known Televangelist." *Journal of Communication and Religion* 14.2 (1991): 44–56.

————. "Sisters of the Spirit: The Rhetorical Method of the Female Faith Healers Aimee Semple McPherson, Kathryn Kuhlman, and Gloria Copeland." *The Journal of Communication and Religion* 16.2 (1993): 111–25.

Stadsklev, Julius. *William Branham, A Prophet Visits South Africa*. Minneapolis: Julius Stadsklev, 1952.

Time. 14 July 1947: 20.

Weaver, C. Douglas. *The Healer Prophet, William Marrion Branham: A Study of the Prophetic in American Pentecostalism*. Macon, GA: Mercer University Press, 1987.

Winans, James A. *Speech Making*. New York: Appleton-Century, 1938.

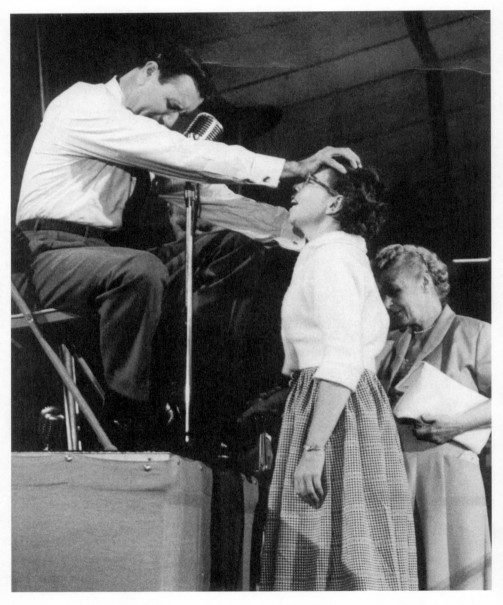

Oral Roberts, June 1957, Trenton, N.J. Courtesy of Oral Roberts Evangelistic Association. Reprinted with permission.

CHAPTER THREE

"God's Man for this Hour": Oral Roberts

Within three years of beginning his independent healing ministry in 1947, Oral Roberts began receiving national media attention. As early as 1951 *Life* magazine suggested that "new revivalist" Oral Roberts had established himself "as a rival of Billy Graham" with his "colorful sermons" and "faith healing" ("A New Revivalist" 73). That same year, in a pictorial essay on Billy Graham, Gayle Jackson, and Oral Roberts, *Look* magazine reported that these men delivered their sermons "with supercharged vigor" bringing "the gospel to life with allegory, colloquialism and a heady dose of dramatics" (Gillenson 84).

As Roberts' reputation grew, so did his media coverage, particularly that of print media. Writing in *Cosmopolitan* magazine in February 1956, Eve Arnold suggested that Oral Roberts' name should be added to the list of prominent American evangelists, which included such well known preachers as Billy Sunday, Aimee Semple McPherson, and Billy Graham (79). Three months later journalist John Kobler wrote in *American* magazine that "Oral Roberts is easily the most sensational soul-saver in the world today" (88). Such notoriety would be commonplace for Roberts during the next five decades of his ministry.

In 1985 Roberts's biographer David Harrell would write of him,

> Oral Roberts has been one of the most influential religious
> leaders in the world in the twentieth century. Roberts
> stands nearer the head of the amorphous [pentecostal]
> movement than any other man, commanding respect
> throughout it. He was the leader of the generation of dy-
> namic revivalists who took the Pentecostal message of heal-
> ing and deliverance around the world in the years after
> 1947. (*Oral Roberts* vii)

For many adults living in the mid to latter half of the twentieth
century, the terms "Oral Roberts" and "faith healing" are synony-
mous, often filled with the image of a tall, handsome man with black,
slicked-back hair laying his hands on some willing individual standing
beneath a chrome microphone in the incandescent lighting of a large
sawdust-strewn canvas tent. But where did he come from? And to
what can we attribute his enormous success?

ROBERTS'S BACKGROUND

Granville Oral Roberts was born in a log cabin near Bebee,
Oklahoma in Pontotoc County on January 24, 1918, the fifth child
and third son of Ellis and Claudius Roberts. Oral's father Ellis was a
poor preacher in the Pentecostal-Holiness denomination (as were
most Pentecostal ministers in his day) who barely eked out a living
either by pasturing small congregations of about ten to twenty people
or by sowing the Pentecostal seed as an itinerant evangelist wherever
he could. Occasionally, Ellis and his family would farm the fields of
neighbors and friends to augment his livelihood (Harrell, *Oral Roberts*
21–25).

After collapsing in the championship game of a high school bas-
ketball tournament in February 1935, the seventeen-year-old Roberts
was diagnosed with tuberculosis. Four months into his agonizing illness, the bed-ridden Roberts was about to undergo a profound spiritual change. One Sunday evening his father, mother, and "nurse"
entered his room. Roberts's father calmly announced, "Oral, I'm going to kneel beside your bed and pray and not stop until you give
your heart to God and get saved." Encircling his bed the three adults
began to pray aloud for Roberts. Roberts recalls, "I raised my head
from the pillow, looked across my body at him kneeling at the foot
of my bed, and saw the big tears rolling down his face." "From the

depths of my soul I called on the name of Jesus for the first time ever to save my soul and my life!" Roberts recalls how he "felt God's presence go through my whole being" (Oral Roberts, *Expect a Miracle* 29–30; Harrell, *Oral Roberts* 32–34).

It was not until the end of July 1935, however, that Roberts claims he was healed of tuberculosis when he attended the revival of a man with a questionable reputation—the nomadic evangelist and faith healer George W. Moncey, who screamed in the face of Roberts that uncharacteristically cool summer evening, "You foul tormenting disease, I command you in the name of Jesus Christ of Nazareth, come out of this boy! Loose him and let him go free" (Oral Roberts, *Expect a Miracle* 33; Harrell, *Oral Roberts* 3–7).

During the remainder of the summer Roberts preached with other young Pentecostal men near Ada, Oklahoma before joining his father in the fall as part of a father-and-son, traveling evangelistic team, although Roberts had not yet received the baptism of the Holy Spirit, something to which all Pentecostals ultimately aspired. That was not to occur until August 1936—the same time he was ordained to preach in the Pentecostal Holiness Church. At the East Oklahoma Conference revival, held in Sulphur, Oklahoma that year, Oral prayed for the baptism in the Holy Spirit and God "baptized me with this mighty experience" (Harrell, *Oral Roberts* 36–39)

For the next five years before taking his first pastorate Oral gained valuable experience preaching as an evangelist. On Christmas Day 1938 he married Evelyn Fahnestock, a Pentecostal girl he met at the East Oklahoma Conference camp meeting in August 1936. After two and a half years as an itinerant husband-and-wife evangelistic team (Evelyn played the piano), Roberts took his first pastorate at Fuquay Springs, North Carolina at the age of twenty-three in November 1941. By the fall of 1946 Roberts had accepted his fourth pastorate at the Pentecostal Holiness Church in Enid, Oklahoma having been the pastor at Shawnee, Oklahoma and Toccoa, Georgia in the interim between his first pastorate and his move to Enid. While at Enid, Oral grew dissatisfied with the lukewarm spirituality of his congregation (Harrell, *Oral Roberts* 47–65).

Although Roberts claims to have received frequent visitations from God as early as 1935, it was not until April 1947, while lying on the floor of the study in his church building in Enid and praying, that according to him God said to him, "From this hour you shall have My power to heal the sick and to cast out demons" (Oral Roberts,

Expect a Miracle 77). That same month he began holding healing services at the church on Sunday afternoons. One of the biggest steps of his healing ministry, however, occurred on May 25, 1947, when he rented the Education Building in downtown Enid. At two o'clock in the afternoon, with 1,200 people present, Roberts held a healing service after preaching his sermon "If You Need Healing—Do These Things." This sermon was later to be published in book form and read by millions. In fact Roberts would eventually offer this booklet to anyone watching his television program who desired to receive a healing. In June 1947 he resigned his pastorate at Enid, moved to Tulsa in July, and began an independent ministry in the dining room of a little house he and Evelyn had purchased on North Main Street. For the next twenty years, Roberts would crisscross the country hold-ing healing revivals in giant tents that would hold anywhere from 2,000 early in his ministry to 18,000 at its peak (Harrell, *Oral Roberts* 66–85; Harrell, "Oral Roberts and the Shaping of American Chris-tianity"; and Oral Roberts, *Twelve Greatest Miracles of My Ministry* 19–28).

Over the span of his fifty-plus years of ministry, Roberts would literally lay hands on over one million people. Millions upon millions more would be vicariously touched by his radio and television pro-grams. Indeed, Roberts may very well be the foremost faith healer of the twentieth century (Harrell, "Oral Roberts and the Shaping of American Christianity"). Without question he is certainly one of the most well-known. His name has become a household word. But why was Oral Roberts so successful, particularly in the roughly twenty years of his tent ministry which spanned from 1947 through 1968? What rhetorical factors helped convince Roberts' followers that mir-acles were for the here and now, that they, too, could lay claim to something almost too good to be true—a personal, miraculous heal-ing sent from none other than God himself? Let us turn first to a discussion of Roberts' audience if we are to understand the answers to these questions.

ROBERTS'S AUDIENCES

As was the case with those in the audience of both Aimee Semple McPherson and William Branham, Roberts preached primarily to a Pentecostal following, especially early in his career as an independent revivalist. Although the makeup of Roberts's audience began to change slightly in the 1960s, involving more blacks and non-Pentecostals, the core of Roberts's tent followers remained predominantly white and Pentecostal. Most were economically, socially, and educationally deprived, although there was an insignificant number of well-to-do professionals and businessmen who also supported him, though these were relatively few. Roberts himself once noted that his audience was composed of those who had "fallen on hard times," in short, those who had business or family problems (Harrell, *Oral Roberts* 90, 110, 256, 286, 477).

Aside from the predominantly poor, uneducated, and socially deprived, Oral was acutely aware that many in his audience were physically and mentally afflicted, in many cases to the point of despair. Roberts saw scores of his followers as "incurably ill" ("Right Believing"). Many, he believed, "in most cases have exhausted the resources of medical science and now their only hope is faith in God" ("The Power of Positive Faith"). It was common for Roberts to preface his prayer lines, which followed his sermons, with comments such as, "People are sick and afflicted and for many of them, God is their only hope. We have many in the prayer line who are here as a last resort" ("Your Guardian Angel"). In fact, Roberts often used the term "last resort" to describe the condition of those in attendance at his revivals. In a Danville, Virginia crusade in 1956, for example, a woman with a ruptured disk in her back and accompanying pain in her left shoulder and arm appeared before Roberts on the healing platform. He explained her situation to the crowd of anxious onlookers as a "last resort because doctors are afraid to operate. She might go blind" ("God Will Speak to You"). Before beginning his prayer line in a Florence, South Carolina crusade in 1955, Roberts explained to his audience, "People are here from all over America, from many states in this nation. Many of them have been given up to die. And this, in some instances, it's their last resort" ("Demons and Deliverance").

Thus, there can be little doubt that Roberts knew well to whom he was preaching and ministering. He was sensitive to the fact that his followers were simple, uneducated, working-class people who had nowhere to turn but to God. Neither the world nor medical science held an attraction for those in Roberts's tents. Roberts once portrayed his constituency as "the simple, uneducated, uninhibited, with few sidelines to whom God means all, and who worship with their hands, feet, and voices" (Harrell, *Oral Roberts* 256). It was to these kinds of people that Roberts knew he was preaching.

ROBERTS'S DISAVOWING OF PERSONAL POWER

One of the first things one notices about Roberts's discourse during the healing portions of his services is the disclaimer that he frequently offered which was common among other healing revivalists before and after him. In no uncertain terms did he explain who was doing the healing. This much he wanted clear to those in attendance and he went to great links to insure that it was not misunderstood. "I'd like to tell you friends as we start praying for the sick tonight," urged Roberts. "I'd like you to understand how God works through me. I am not the healer. I cannot heal. Only God can do that. But I am an instrument in his hands, which he is using to bring healing to many, many people" ("Right Believing"). As was common in many crusades, during his meetings in Sydney, Australia in 1956, in which he came under fierce attack from the media (Harrell, *Oral Roberts* 73–79), Roberts reminded those in attendance, "God heals. I don't. I am an instrument that God is using, but it's faith in God that heals. I cannot heal, but God can. I lay my hand upon you as a point of contact" ("Miracle Days Are Here Again"). Elsewhere he told an audience, "You may have confidence in my prayers, but your faith must be in God, not in Oral Roberts, not in any one else" ("Making Your Believing a Definite Act of Faith"; see also *Venture into Faith*). On one occasion when the pastor of a Baptist church from Norfolk, Virginia entered Roberts's healing line, Roberts in typical fashion said to him, "Well, brother Brooks, I'd be the last one in the world to claim the gift of healing, but I do believe God has anointed me to pray for the sick" ("God Will Speak to You").

Time after time Roberts emphasized to his audiences that it was God's power that heals people, not his own. Such disavowing of personal power served two rhetorical purposes for Roberts: (1) it demonstrated a sense of humility to his Pentecostal audiences, further endearing himself to them; and (2) ultimately it freed him from critics who were quick to point out when an individual was not healed. Roberts could always say that he was not the source of healing, that he never claimed to be in the first place. Moreover, Roberts often warned people that if they were to be healed, it would have to be a result of their own faith in God. "God is waiting on you to release your faith," he often insisted ("Right Believing"). Obviously then, if no healing occurred the problem lay with the one being healed, not with God or with Oral Roberts.

ROBERTS'S USE OF TESTIMONIES

If Roberts was good at repudiating personal ability to heal people, he was equally adept at employing testimony to persuade his constituency. Though not in every sermon or healing line, Roberts frequently reminded his audiences that: (1) he had been personally called by God; and (2) that he himself had received a personal miracle. On one occasion, for example, he told an Anaheim, California audience, "And you know, in nineteen hundred and forty-seven when the Lord spoke to me and said, 'Son from this hour you will heal the sick and cast out devils by my power,' I had no conception of the immensity of God's plan. . . . I didn't know that I would stand up and I could say that healing is for everybody" ("Healing Is Not a Luxury"). On another occasion he told an audience, "The Lord said to me, 'From this hour, you'll cast out demons and heal the sick by my power.' . . . This is something I cannot explain. It came to me by the power of God. And I've prayed for thousands upon thousands of these cases and in many instances the Lord has set them free and made them whole" ("Demons and Deliverance"). The fact is God often spoke to Roberts and Roberts often reminded his audiences of his conversations with God. In this way he convinced many of his Pentecostal followers who already believed in the miraculous to accept the idea that they could receive their healing because "God's man for this hour" was bringing deliverance to his generation ("Your Guardian Angel").

Although often the two ideas were disclosed at the same time, when Roberts was not reminding his audience that God had called him, he was informing them of how God had healed him. This personal testimony was one he would echo thousands of times throughout his career. In the healing line of one of his crusades early in his tent ministry a lady came forward to be healed of tuberculosis. Roberts reminded her, "I was healed of tuberculosis myself" ("Right Believing"). When a young boy who stuttered entered the healing line,

Roberts reminded the boy of his own condition before he was healed: "You know when I was your age . . . I stammered real bad and if my teacher gave us a test and let us write the answers I'd make a good grade, but if she said you had to come up and recite, I was dead. I could not talk" ("The Truth about God"). Once when asked by the popular talk-show host Merv Griffin what was the greatest miracle of his "entire ministry," Roberts responded, "Merv . . . the greatest miracle I ever saw was my own personal miracle when God healed me of tuberculosis and loosed my stammering tongue. It was the greatest because it happened to me" (*Twelve Greatest Miracles of My Ministry* 7).

Personal testimonies such as these vividly pointed out to an audience: (1) that Roberts believed in what he preached to others because healing happened to him; and (2) if God could heal Roberts, He could heal anyone. Or as Roberts once told his followers after disclosing to them that God had healed him of tuberculosis and stuttering, "what Christ has done for me, he can do for you." In essence Roberts was living proof that "God is a good God" who would heal the mentally and physically distressed (*Venture into Faith*).

More often than recounting his own life's story, Roberts would generally rely on the testimony of those in his healing lines. In a Winston-Salem, North Carolina crusade in 1955, for instance, a sixty-four-year-old "skeptic," who came from New York to be healed of his cancer testified that he became a believer after he "saw the film from the tent." Roberts laid his hands on the man's head and prayed for him. When asked by Roberts why he "jerked," the man responded, "A thrill went right through me." When asked how he knew he had been healed, the man answered, "I feel fine. I feel wonderful" ("Your Guardian Angel").

In addition to using the immediate testimony of people in healing lines, as in the above example, Roberts often brought people back into the healing line who had been healed in a previous service to testify about their healing. In an Austin, Texas crusade in 1957 Fred Odel from Oakland, California, who had been healed of "cancer of the lung and lymph glands" at an Oral Roberts crusade on "April 5, 1955, at 8:30 p.m. in Jacksonville, Florida," brought an envelope containing a letter from a doctor and x-rays to prove that his cancer was "completely gone." "That's my proof," said Odel when asked what was in the envelope. Odel asserted that he had been in many churches since 1955 "testifying for the Lord's healing." When asked by Roberts if he would like to say anything to the crowd, Odel turned to the audience and pleaded, "Have faith in God. God was my last resort. I just turned loose and let go and let God" ("Making Your Believing a Definite Act of Faith").

In a 1964 crusade in St. Petersburg, Florida a Reverend Banks stood before Oral Roberts to testify about how God had healed him of a lung disease on July 11, 1962, at an Oral Roberts crusade in Irving, Texas. "What would you say to someone who wanted to be healed?" queried Roberts. "Brother Roberts, I'd like to say this tonight," continued Banks. "Certainly a person has got to realize that they have to turn to God. There is no other that can do the healing except God. We must believe. We must have faith in God. I believe we all have a certain amount of faith, but we've got to exercise that faith. We've got to put it to use tonight. Simply trust God. Read his word and believe and it will be done" ("The Hands of God").

Time after time Roberts brought back people into his healing line who had been healed in some previous crusade. He understood the value of personal testimony and was willing to use it to convince his followers that they too could receive their own miracle.

EMPIRICAL PROOFS: SEEING IS BELIEVING

If the personal testimony of either Roberts or the one in the healing line were not enough to convince onlookers that they could receive a miracle, surely a physical demonstration would more than suffice. And Roberts was always willing to accommodate his equally eager audience with some "empirical proof."

After ostensibly healing a boy with a limp in his left leg during one crusade, Roberts asked his associate minister Bob Deweese to put the boy on stage so that everyone could see how the limp had left him. Then he directed the boy to walk to the end of the ramp to demonstrate how straight he could walk. After doing so, the audience erupted in applause as Oral yelled, "Isn't that wonderful?" ("Your Guardian Angel").

During the same crusade a lady stood before Roberts to be healed of sugar diabetes and a goiter in the neck—an ailment often healed in Roberts's crusades. After laying his hands on the woman to be healed, Oral pinched the woman's skin from her throat and told her that her goiter was leaving because her skin was "loose and flabby." Then, turning toward the audience, Roberts explained how the

woman's neck was "as smooth as it can be" ("Your Guardian Angel").
Whether it was asking someone with a back problem to bend over
and touch his toes, someone with a "dislocated hip" to raise it up and
down for the audience to examine, or some other similar demonstration, Oral loved to prove empirically how God was moving in the
lives of people under his tent ("Healing Is Not a Luxury"). Convinced
that such strategy worked, Roberts boldly appealed to his television
viewers, "Now after you've seen with your own eyes and felt with
your own heart what God's done for the people in the healing line
tonight, I want to offer prayer for you personally there in your room
for the Lord to heal you" ("Demons and Deliverance").

ROBERTS'S RELIANCE ON SCRIPTURE

Of all rhetorical strategies available to him, perhaps none would
be as persuasive to Roberts's followers as his constant reference to
miracles in the Bible. For Roberts every idea ultimately revolved
around whether it was first revealed in the scriptures. Without the
Bible perhaps all other forms of proof would be useless for it was the
Bible that, in Roberts's mind, served as the foundation for miracles
in the first place. There can be little doubt that, had it not been for
the Bible's discussion of the miraculous, Roberts would never have
even broached the subject with his congregation in April 1947.

Roberts recalls how in that year at the age of twenty-nine and a
half, he "began a study of the Bible as I never had before." Focusing
primarily on "the Four Gospels and the book of Acts," he concluded
that there was a "gap between what I saw Jesus Christ to be in the
now and what I saw people's understanding of Him to be. I saw what
Jesus had done 2,000 years ago and was present to do in my generation, and . . . that He would actually do the same things. . . ." As a
result of studying the scriptures, Roberts had convinced himself that
"Jesus came to deliver and heal the people . . . to set them free . . . to
give them abundant life in the now of their existence!!! I saw that
Jesus was always in the now—the same yesterday, today and forever"—a paraphrase of Hebrews 13:8 (Oral Roberts, *Twelve Greatest
Miracles of My Ministry* 19–20).

Frequently citing Hebrews 13:8 Roberts reminded his audiences
that Jesus was essentially the same in Oral's day as He was when He
was alive nearly two thousand years ago. "Jesus Christ is the same
yesterday, today and forever," Roberts often told his followers

("Healing Is Not a Luxury"; "The Power of Positive Faith"). Even into the late 1980s, Roberts articulated, "What Jesus was then he is now" (*Venture into Faith*).

Over and over again Oral alluded to passage after passage in the New Testament where Jesus healed people. Roberts would draw on verses such as Mark 16:15–16 ("Miracle Days Are Here Again"), Mark 9:23 ("Making Your Believing a Definite Act of Faith"), and Matthew 10:1–7 and 12:43 ("Demons and Deliverance") to name a few. On one occasion Roberts boasted that Matthew 8:5–13 was "the greatest healing chapter in the Bible" (*Venture in Faith*). Leaving his audience with the impression that he was well versed in the Scriptures, Roberts reminded his audience that there were only two people in the entire New Testament whom Jesus commended for their great faith: (1) the Roman Centurion of Matthew 8, whose servant was healed of palsy, and (2) the Syrophoenician woman of Matthew 15, whose daughter was delivered from a demon ("Healing Is Not a Luxury"). In making statements like this, Roberts raised his credibility and hence persuasiveness.

If as contemporary rhetorical theorist Alan Monroe argues, "knowledge, self-confidence, and skill . . . form the basis for effective speech" (Monroe 7), there can be little doubt as to why Roberts was a successful preacher because he sounded to his Pentecostal audience as if he knew everything there was to know about miracles in the Bible, leaving the impression that he had spent long hours studying the issue, which indeed he had. Moreover, he preached his message in a confident manner. Harrell argues that after hearing one of Roberts's sermons his Pentecostal audience left "with the indelible impression that they had sat at the feet of a scholar" (Harrell, *Oral Roberts* 477).

Because an argument is only as good as a speaker's audience will allow it to be, Roberts was not compelled to demonstrate how the scriptures he employed supported his claims of the miraculous. His audiences had never been critical listeners. Hence, Roberts's audiences saw no discrepancy in what they read about Jesus doing and what they saw in Roberts's crusades. All they knew was that Roberts was supporting his actions, in large part, merely by referring to examples in the New Testament and this was good enough for them. They never stopped to question the relevance of these Biblical examples to their day because Jesus was supposed to be the same yesterday, today, and forever which Oral never ceased to remind them.

ROBERTS, THE MASTER STORYTELLER

In one of his "seven lamps of speechmaking," William Norwood Brigance, a rhetorical theorist whose work overlapped the preaching of Oral Roberts, advised that since "listeners think in images; be therefore specific, pictorial, and vivid" (175). One way to do this, reveals Brigance, is to use illustrations for audiences love to hear stories (256). He suggests that a good illustration "has suspense that makes people want to listen in order to find out what happened" (238). "Illustrations are the most powerful form of support yet discovered by man" (256).

Almost as if he were taking a cue from Brigance himself, Roberts masterfully told stories, drawing in audiences as he attempted to prove his points through illustrations. Harrell argues that, "In many ways, his [Roberts's] illustrations were what gripped his audiences . . ." (*Oral Roberts* 478). After reading Biblical stories, Roberts would immediately recount the story in his own words, adding verve to make the story come alive. Once, for example, when preaching his sermon "The Power of Positive Faith" in 1954, Roberts began in typical fashion by reading a text from the scriptures, in this case, the story of David slaying a lion and the giant Goliath (II Sam. 17:32–36). Upon finishing his reading Roberts began retelling the story in his own words, gesturing with his hands as if he were the shepherd boy David grabbing the lion by his beard with one hand and smiting it with his other hand. Roberts then proceeded to retell how David slew Goliath, acting out physically the throwing of a stone around his head in slingshot fashion. In a word, Roberts's storytelling was engaging, illustrating through story how a positive faith can bring about positive results in a person's life.

If not retelling some story found in the Bible, Roberts was usually supporting some point with a real-life secular example. Once, for instance, in trying to impress upon his audience the beauty and significance of "the hands of God," Oral told of a woman who rescued her infant daughter from the flames of a house fire. In the process the woman's hands were badly burned and disfigured. Consequently, she wore gloves to keep from embarrassing her daughter as her daughter grew older. One day, however, the mother forgot to wear her gloves at her daughter's birthday party which humiliated the young girl in front of her friends. The mother sat the girl down and told her how it was that she had come to have scarred hands, at which point the daughter took the mother's hands and kissed them and told her mother that she had "the most beautiful hands in the world." In dramatic fashion Oral proceeded to draw the analogy to Christ, concluding that the hands of Christ, pierced with nail wounds, are beautiful to Christians ("The Hands of God").

When not using Biblical examples or real-life illustrations, Roberts would often employ hypothetical stories to prove his points. Once, for example, he told of three people trying to enter heaven. The first person was a retired military general who urged Saint Peter to allow him in on the basis that he had fought for religious freedom. Since the general gave the wrong "password," he was "banished." The second individual to approach Saint Peter was a rich man who tried to enter heaven on the basis of how much he had given to the poor. Like the general, he too, was turned away. Finally, a little old woman came to Saint Peter, singing about the blood of Christ having cleansed her. Roberts narrated how the gates of heaven immediately "flew open wide" and the "hosts of heaven" joined her in song ("Oral Roberts's Million Souls Crusade"). Roberts used this story to support the idea that a person is saved by grace and not by works. Not only did the story act as proof of an idea, but the interest appeal helped to grab and maintain the audience's attention.

ROBERTS'S ORGANIZATION

In addition to the above, one factor that contributed to Roberts's appeal as a speaker was his excellent organizational skills. While there exists a number of videotaped sermons with no discernible organizational structure, it is common to hear Roberts clearly delineate the main points in many of his lessons, preaching on topics such as four powers Christ gave over demons ("Demons and Deliverance") or three ways to exercise one's faith in God ("Making Your Believing a Definite Act of Faith").

Harrell suggests that Roberts's sermons were more structured than those of other Pentecostal preachers, probably as a result of his study of homiletics at Oklahoma Baptist University. Certainly they were more organized than that of any other faith healer in this book. Harrell also notes that it was his organization and content, unlike other Pentecostal oratory, that initially "thrust Oral to the fore of the heal-

ing revival and gained the respect of the Pentecostal subculture."
There can be little doubt that such orderly three- and four-point
sermons, often prepared on hotel stationery, greatly contributed to
Roberts's credibility as a preacher (*Oral Roberts* 476–77).

Perhaps no better example of Roberts's ability to organize is seen
in his sermon "Why You Should Get Saved." One by one Roberts
clearly articulates three reasons why one should accept Christ: "You
should get saved first because getting saved is the only power in the
whole world . . . that can blot out your sins and can wash your soul
whiter than snow." After discussing this point, Roberts transitioned
to his next point: "Second, you should get saved because then Jesus
will carry your heavy load." Finally after a discussion of point two,
Roberts transitioned, "Third, you should get saved because getting
saved breaks the hold that hell has on you and causes heaven to begin
in your soul" ("Why You Should Get Saved").

Not only does the above example illustrate Roberts's ability to organize, but it also demonstrates his use of parallelism. According to
contemporary rhetorical theorist Alan Monroe, a speaker should "try
to use the same sentence structure and a similar type of phraseology
in each of a series of main points." "Since these points represent
coordinate major units of your speech," suggests Monroe, "word
them so they sound that way" (267). Whether realizing it or not,
Roberts often followed Monroe's advice.

In addition to good organization, occasionally detected through
parallelism, Roberts often excelled in signposting. Signposting is the
numerical announcing of a main point to be discussed. Contemporary
rhetorical theorist Allan Monroe argues that in trying to make tran-
sitions between main points clear, the speaker may "even go so far
as to enumerate your points, 'First, second, third, etc.' " (389). As one
can see from the above example, such a practice was not foreign to
Roberts.

ROBERTS'S STYLE

Perhaps one of Roberts's greatest assets as a preacher was the style
in which he preached. He was very interesting to listen to because he
was forceful yet conversational. His words flowed freely, revealing a
cadence or rhythm pleasing to the ear. And, although he spoke with
a "broad Okie drawl," his language was generally free of mispro-

nounced words and grammatical errors, unlike that of his counterpart William Branham (Harrell, *Oral Roberts* 195).

Roberts often employed repetition in his preaching. Repetition involves the repeated use of a word or group of words for the sake of emphasis. Rhetorical theorists have long recognized the value of repetition in public speaking. McBurney and Wrage, for instance, suggest that a speaker's repetition "adds clarity and emphasis" (157). Brigance argues that "repetition drives an ideal home. It reinforces memory" (262). Apparently Roberts was aware of this advantage, for he frequently used repetition in his preaching. On one occasion Roberts preached, "Let Jesus take that burden. Let Jesus take that heavy load. Let the carpenter of Nazareth make a new yoke for your souls" ("Why You Should Get Saved"). "See the power of this great God. See the power of God as it is exemplified in his creative processes and power. See the power of this limitless being," he once admonished an audience ("The Truth about God"). In one sermon in which he tried to argue why everyone should be healed, Roberts contested in repetitive fashion, "It is not the bread of the wicked. It is not the bread of the sinner. It is not the bread of the fool who says there is no God. It is the bread of the children" ("Healing Is Not a Luxury"). Once, in reaching a climatic point, Roberts characteristically used repetition when he screamed, "Yes again, miracle days are here. Miracle days for me. Miracle days for you. Miracle days for everybody in the world" ("Miracle Days Are Here Again"). Such repetition alone was often enough to convince his followers that miracles and healing were available to anyone who chose to believe, and practically every sermon he preached contained one or more instances of repetition.

Another stylistic trait of Roberts's sermons was the character dialogue which he employed during his storytelling. In other words, when relaying such illustrations, Roberts often took on the persona of the characters within his stories, employing direct quotations of these characters to relay them. In illustrating a point about why one should "get saved," Roberts once told the story of two men, one "unsaved" and one "saved" with whom he had prior conversations. Mimicking the "unsaved" man, Roberts narrated how he confessed to "living in hell." The "saved" man, however, disclosed, "Brother Roberts, I feel like I'm in heaven" ("Why You Should Get Saved"). Roberts conveyed the unsaved man's words in a bitter tone but the saved man's dialogue in a pleasant, almost care-free manner, much as the men themselves originally spoke to Roberts. Such dramatizing of characters, which Roberts often did, merely added interest appeal to an already inherently interesting story.

A final stylistic trait that made Roberts so attractive to people was his sense of humor. Audiences often chuckled at things he would say either while preaching or performing in the healing lines. On one occasion, for instance, after a boy's neck and nostrils were supposedly healed, Roberts asked him how he felt. Roberts made the audience laugh when he repeated in a humorous, effeminate voice the boy's words "lovely, good" to describe his condition ("Miracle Days Are Here Again"). Harrell tells of a time when a seventy-five-year-old woman came into one of Roberts's healing lines for a "general over-haul." Roberts humorously replied, "You want to be 16 again? . . . Well, the Lord may not make you 16, but He may make you a young 75" (*Oral Roberts* 102). If as Brigance argues, "a sense of humor is enduring. It wins the sympathy of those who listen. It earns respect from those who disagree. It leaves a friendly, lingering memory. . . ." (82) then there can be little wonder why Roberts endeared himself to his Pentecostal audiences time and time again. He had the enviable ability to make them laugh.

ROBERTS'S MEMORY AND DELIVERY

Oral Roberts neither memorized his speeches nor spoke from notes. He did speak extemporaneously, however. Brigance informs us that a "true extemporaneous speech . . . is a speech in which the ideas are firmly fixed in mind, but the exact words are not memorized" (61). This was precisely the way Roberts spoke. Monroe argues that a carefully developed extemporaneous speech "will result in a speech nearly as polished as a memorized one and certainly more vigorous, flexible, and spontaneous" (155). The effect that such a speech would have on an audience's perception of the speaker is evident. What audience would not want to listen to a "vigorous, flexible, and spon-taneous" speech?

Videotaped sermons show that Roberts had exceptional recall of the main points of his sermons as well as any supporting materials he might employ, such as anecdotes, examples, or scriptural references. Harrell suggests that Roberts had "an insatiable need to feel his au-diences in personal encounter" and quotes Roberts as saying, "when I walk up there I don't want anything but you on my mind. I want to preach to you, with your need, because I want my needs met. . . . It's an act of love" (*Oral Roberts* 478). It was for these reasons that he refused to use notes.

During his tent campaigns of the 1950s and 1960s, Roberts's associate pastor Bob Deweese would introduce him: "And now ladies and gentlemen, it's my happy privilege and pleasure to present the man that God has raised up with a message for your deliverance, God's man for this hour, the Reverend Oral Roberts" (see "Your Guardian Angel" or "Making Your Believing a Definite Act of Faith," for example). After this introduction, Roberts would bound onto the platform through a door at the back of the stage. He always entered with a spring in his step and a smile on his face. What the audience saw was a tall (around 6'2"), handsome, neatly combed, black-haired, well-dressed man wearing a light-colored suit, white shirt, and dark tie with a gold tie clip. Frequently he would lead the audience in a hymn, after which he would ask them to turn and shake hands with "three neighbors." Once the audience had a chance to settle in, Roberts would proceed by reading the Biblical text of his lesson. Usually upon the completion of the reading, he would recount the story in his own words, and then announce the point of his sermon, something like, "And now I'd like to speak to you on the power of positive faith" ("The Power of Positive Faith"; "Right Believing"). After announcing the title of his sermon, he would launch into the first of the three or four points he had planned to discuss.

After a few minutes into his lesson Roberts would raise his volume, speaking loudly. Often he placed his left hand in his left coat pocket, occasionally took it out and picked up the chrome microphone stand as he walked to the right or left on the platform ("The Power of Positive Faith"). Once he was warmed up, Roberts would thrust his hand into the air or place them on his hips before he picked up the microphone and moved it around and constantly paced across the stage. By this point his long, black hair had usually fallen out of place over his forehead. All the while, Roberts was never at a loss for words. In fact, it's hard to imagine a speaker with more dynamism and fluency than Oral had during his tent crusades ("Your Guardian Angel").

CONCLUSION

In summary Oral Roberts was an excellent orator and persuader. Not only was his content compelling as he relied on testimonies, storytelling, and references to scripture, but the manner in which he presented his material was nothing short of captivating. While one may not agree with his theology, he or she is compelled to give Roberts high marks for his rhetorical ability. He provided both style and substance, form and content wherever and whenever he preached.

If, as Aristotle notes, ethos or speaker credibility might very well be the speaker's single most potent appeal to move an audience (25), then certainly Roberts was not lacking in this area. He had high ethos with his Pentecostal followers. He appeared competent, he was morally upright, he conveyed good will toward his audiences, and he was dynamic, all of which contributed to his rhetorical reputation. As I have noted at the beginning of this chapter, such credibility did not go unnoticed even by many secular observers who followed either out of simple curiosity or duty as a reporter.

Given Roberts's rhetorical prowess, there can be little doubt as to why he became as successful as he did during his lifetime. While this was not the only talent on which he built his success, it surely was one of the pillars. For, without the ability to move large audiences early in his career through his preaching and healing, he would have been unable to secure the financial and moral support so desperately needed to sustain such an influential ministry over the next fifty years of his life.

REFERENCES

Aristotle. *The Rhetoric*. Trans. W. Rhys Roberts. New York: Modern Library, 1954.

Arnold, Eve. "The Laying on of Hands." *Cosmopolitan* Feb. 1956: 78–83.

Brigance, William Norwood. *Speech: Its Techniques and Disciplines in a Free Society*. 2nd ed. New York: Appleton-Century-Crofts, 1961.

Gillenson, Lewis W. "The Summer Sawdust Trail." *Look* 31 July 1951: 84–89.

Harrell, David Edwin. *Oral Roberts: An American Life*. Bloomington, IN: Indiana University Press, 1985.

———. "Oral Roberts and the Shaping of American Christianity." The Oxford Lecture Series. 5 April 1984.

Kobler, John. "Oral Roberts: King of the Faith Healers." *American* May 1956: 20–21, 88–90.

McBurney, James H. and Ernest J. Wrage. *The Art of Good Speech*. New York: Prentice-Hall, 1964.

Monroe, Alan H. *Principles and Types of Speech*. 4th ed. New York: Scott, Foresman, and Co., 1955.

"A New Revivalist." *Life* 30 May 1951: 73–74, 76–78.

"Oral Roberts' Million Souls Crusade." Milwaukee, WI. April, 1956. *Chronicles of Faith*. KWMI. Tulsa, OK. May 24, 1996.

Roberts, Oral. "Demons and Deliverance." Sermon. Florence, S.C. 1955.

———. *Expect a Miracle: My Life and Ministry*. Nashville: Thomas Nelson, 1995.

———. "God Will Speak to You." Sermon. Danville, VA. 1956.

———. "The Hands of God." Sermon. St. Petersburg, FL. 1964.

———. "Healing is Not a Luxury." Sermon. Anaheim, CA. 1955.

———. "Making Your Believing a Definite Act of Faith." Sermon. Austin, TX. 1957.

———. "Miracle Days Are Here Again." Sermon. Sydney, Australia. 1956.

———. "The Power of Positive Faith." Sermon. Phoenix, AZ. 1954.

———. "Right Believing: The Master Key to Healing." Sermon. Portland, OR. 1954.

———. "The Truth about God." Sermon. Eugene, OR. 1958.

———. *Twelve Greatest Miracles of My Ministry*. Tulsa, OK: Pinoak Publications, 1974.

———. "Why You Should Get Saved." Sermon. Billings, MO. 1955.

———. "Your Guardian Angel." Sermon. Winston-Salem, NC. 1955.

Venture into Faith. Prod. and Dir. Herb A. Lightman. 1952. Archangel Motion Pictures. 1987.

Asa Alonzo Allen, ca. 1960. Courtesy of The Flower Pentecostal Heritage Center. Reprinted with permission.

CHAPTER FOUR

"God's Man of Faith and Power": Asa Alonzo Allen

Some saw him as a heavy-drinking con-artist whose mission was to swindle his audience out of their money any way he could. He has been described as a "notorious revivalist" and "huckster" who "scammed his followers" by claiming he could either turn one dollar bills into twenties, cure individuals by sending them prayer cloths anointed with oil, or raise the dead (Hanegraaff 2–3; Harrell, 72, 199–200).

Others, however, saw him as a devout man of God who cast out demons, made people well, or brought about some other good. To many, if anybody were on God's side, certainly it was the Reverend A. A. Allen. Lewis points out that while many "reviled" him, by the close of the 1950s Asa Alonzo Allen had become "one of the most popular [and] revered . . . faith healers in the country" (168). At Allen's memorial service on June 15, 1970, longtime associate Raymond Hoekstra referred to him as "one of the most remarkable men I've ever known." Kent Rogers, who joined A. A. Allen as song leader and co-evangelist in 1954, suggested that there "will never be another A. A. Allen. No one person can ever take his place. No one else can ever do what he did." Allen's tombstone would eventually eulogize him as "God's Man of Faith and Power," the title used by either R. W. Schambach or Kent Rogers to introduce him to his audiences at his revivals (Stewart 1, 8, 16–18).

But whatever he was labeled—whether good or bad—A. A. Allen turned heads and raised eyebrows wherever his popular tent revival and healing campaign took him. In a story on Allen published late in his career in 1969, *Look* magazine called him a "mogul" in "the God business," suggesting he is "the nation's topmost tent-toting, old-fashioned evangelical roarer" (Hedgepeth 24–25). *Time* once referred to him as a "fire-breathing evangelist and faith healer." The *Los Angeles Times* suggested that he "was among the last of the oldtime, fire and brimstone traveling evangelists" (Stewart 8).

There can be no doubt that Asa Alonzo Allen, or "Triple A" as he was occasionally called, was one of the most colorful faith healers (a label he despised) of the entire twentieth century. Certainly he was one of the most lively and unforgettable healing revivalists to emerge following World War II. Melton, Lucas, and Stone suggest that "In spite of his obvious shortcomings, Allen is remembered today as one of the most influential healing evangelists of his era" (3). Throughout his career, thousands upon thousands flocked yearly to his crusades, whether held in tents large enough to cover a football field or in large metropolitan auditoriums.

Describing the time when he first laid eyes on Allen as a "shining moment," Associate Minister and protégé Don Stewart recounts that he was "a trim man, about five feet eight with a broad, warm smile. His hair was almost as red as his [new red 1956 Cadillac] car." Because of slight physical resemblances, Allen was occasionally referred to as "the Spike Jones of the pulpit" or "the James Cagney of the sawdust trail" (Stuart 8, 58). *Look* magazine once described him as "a garish leprechaun (in a snazzy clash of camel-colored suit, yellow shirt and orange tie)" (Hedgepeth 24).

BEGINNINGS

A. A. Allen was born in Sulphur Rock, Arkansas on March 27, 1911. The last of seven children born to alcoholic parents, Leona Magdalene Clark and Asa Alonso Allen, Allen had learned to drink before the age of five and smoke before the age of six. After his mother divorced his father and married a tall, mulatto man named John Bailey, who also drank heavily, Allen moved with them from Batesville, Arkansas to Carthage, Missouri.

Raised in poverty, early in life he learned to steal anything from apples and pears to chickens in order to survive. At eleven Allen attempted to run away from home to be with his natural father but failed. Eventually he succeeded at the age of fourteen, the same year he dropped out of the eighth grade out of shame for not having shoes to wear. He recounts how he lost his "sexual purity" around the age of twelve. "By the time I was eighteen," he discloses, "I no longer went out with girls. I didn't have to. I was tied to one woman. I had taken a common-law wife. She was a married woman ten years my senior" (Allen and Wagner 40–62).

During the depression Allen spent ninety days in a county jail for stealing sacks of corn from a farmer's field. He describes himself at the age of twenty-three as "an ex-jail bird drifting aimlessly through life." "I had the reputation . . . of being the worst sinner that anyone knew . . ." (Allen and Wagner 63–64).

Things began to look up, however, for Allen. At the age of twenty-three, he visited a revival held by a woman preacher named Nina DePriestes at the Onward Methodist Church. During the second night of the revival on June 4, 1934, Allen answered the altar call. "God saved me in a moment," he suggests. "And there in church, in front of everyone, I cried like a baby. I had never bawled that much in my life." A week later he was baptized (Allen and Wagner 68–71).

Shortly after his salvation Allen attended a revival in Mt. Vernon, Missouri held in the home of a "Brother Hunter," a Pentecostal deacon. There he discovered that Pentecostals "were on fire, really aflame for the Lord." After a two-week membership, he left the Methodist church and joined Hunter's Pentecostal congregation. By now the two had become close friends. In time Allen accompanied Brother Hunter to a Pentecostal camp meeting held at Miami, Oklahoma. Two nights before the end of the revival, Allen received the baptism of the Holy Spirit after answering the altar call. After working a year and a half on a ranch in Colorado, where he preached to fence posts and livestock, he moved back to Missouri and began preaching wherever he could find an audience (Allen and Wagner 80–82).

Eventually Allen was licensed to preach in 1936 by the Assemblies of God, the same year he married his wife Lexie, whom he would eventually divorce in 1962 for mental cruelty. After years of itinerant preaching, fraught with financial insecurity, in 1947 he took the pastorate of an Assemblies of God congregation in Corpus Christi, Texas. In 1949, however, he quit his position and decided to return to the road as a traveling evangelist after being inspired by Oral Roberts at one of his crusades. In truth, the fact that his church board decided not to sponsor a radio program he wanted to produce also contributed to his resignation (Harrell 67–68; Lewis 165; Morris 50; Simson 99).

Allen believed that in order for his revival to flourish he needed to buy a tent. "The evangelists who were drawing the largest audiences were doing so under tents . . . that spread their wings over thousands at each meeting," he argued. "I felt the Lord wanted me to have a tent, too. . . ." Allen purchased his first tent in 1951 from Jack Coe, another popular faith healer, for $8,500. Having only $1,500 as a down payment, Allen agreed to pay $100 "every night I used the tent until the balance was met." Shortly after he purchased his tent, Allen bought "two old trucks" for $2,000 to haul it around the country. He pitched his first revival tent on July 4, 1951, in Yakima, Washington (Allen and Wagner 128–33; Lewis 166). For the next several years he would crisscross America holding revivals wherever he could draw a crowd. In the winter Allen would pitch his tent in Florida occasionally holding revivals in Cuba. As late as 1965 Allen also preached in England and Wales, although the crowds there were not as receptive as those in America and Cuba (Lewis 169).

After setting up his headquarters in Dallas in 1953, he began a radio program entitled "The Allen Revival Hour." (Eventually, he would have a television program by the same name.) (Harrell 67–68). By December 1959 Allen's radio program was carried on nearly sixty stations across America (*Miracle Magazine* Dec. 1959, 13). Ten years later not only was Allen still broadcasting on close to sixty stations but his new weekly television program "Miracles Today" was aired on forty-three stations ("Faith Healers" 64).

Trouble rocked Allen's popular ministry in the mid-fifties. On October 21, 1955, he was arrested for drunk driving in Knoxville, Tennessee. Allen recounted that he had been kidnapped and knocked unconscious. According to Allen, when he regained consciousness in a back room, someone was pouring liquor down his throat. Many people, including high-ranking officials in the Assemblies of God, were incredulous about Allen's story, especially since Allen forfeited his bond and did not appear in court. Shortly thereafter, the Assemblies of God denomination disfellowshipped him (Harrell 70–71; Lewis 167).

While Allen did lose some followers over this ordeal, many of the faithful continued to admire him. In the fall of 1956 Allen began an independent ministry known as the "Miracle Revival Fellowship." That same year he began publication of *Miracle Magazine*, which had a subscription of over 200,000 at the end of its first year (Lewis 167). Well into the next decade, Allen remained popular among thousands of original loyal supporters. In fact Allen had such a large following that he was able to finance Miracle Valley in 1958, a 2,500 acre complex near Bisbee, Arizona replete with a Bible College, radio and television stations, a recording studio, a print shop, and a retirement community, among other facilities. According to Allen, at one time he received "close to 400,000 letters a year from ninety countries." Hundreds in need of healing and prayer called Allen's twenty-four hour switchboard daily (Allen and Wagner 181; *This Is Miracle Valley Video*).

On June 11, 1970, Allen was found dead in his underwear, slumped over a table in his room at the Jack Tar Hotel in San Francisco. A Miracle Valley spokesperson reported to the Associated Press that the cause of Allen's death was a heart attack, but citing a coroner's report, a United Press International article dated June 25, 1970, reported that Allen had died of alcoholism and liver failure. Authorities found several bottles of pills in his room along with over $2,000 in his wallet. Ironically, the same day he died, radio audiences, unaware that they were listening to taped messages, were assured by Allen himself that despite rumors of his demise, he was very much alive and well. The reality was that Allen had already departed this life (Morris 50–51; see also "Reverend A. A. Allen, Evangelist, Dies").

Among many, Allen will always be remembered most for the Knoxville incident. However, despite whatever problems may have plagued his ministry in 1955 and the years following, he continued to be immensely popular. But how was it that he, like McPherson, Branham, and Roberts, symbolically induced his audience to accept his message of the miraculous? And what was it like to sit through one of Allen's sermons and subsequent healing sessions?

ALLEN'S AUDIENCE

In addition to pictures as they appeared on television and in magazines, journalistic accounts of those in Allen's audiences provide us with a clear understanding of those to whom he preached. *Look* magazine described Allen's followers as "an elderly woman with stringy gray hair down to her waist and tight-clenched old eyes . . . skeletal men in bib overalls, chubby matrons, scrawny teenies and septuage-narians." Moreover, they were described as "jut-jawed old black men; bearded women; dwarfs; blind ladies; men with giant goiters; lay preachers; lunatics; splayed feet; faded eyes; tight skirts and teased-up hair; varicose veins; hook hands; work shirts; [and] calico. . . ." Allen's followers were individuals of all ages and races with "bottomless frus-trations" and "unlabeled loneliness"—"a need for some faint color-ation to the grayness of their days" (*Hedgepeth* 24, 28).

Like McPherson, Branham, and Roberts, Allen was also well ac-quainted with his constituency. Often, for example, he would say of someone who came to his revivals seeking help, "The doctors say there's nothing more they can do. They've given him up. They say there's nothing more for him to do than starve to death" (*Miracles Today*). Near the end of one of his television programs Allen in-structed, "This is our prayer of faith for the sick, for the suffering— and as I always say—oft times the dying because hundreds of people are rolled under this tent on this ramp on stretchers in dying con-dition" ("Allen Exhorting"; "It Is Finished").

In addition to the physically broken Allen consciously reached out to blacks. "The real move to God today is among the colored peo-ple," boasted Allen. "The Scripture says the common people received Him gladly, referring to Jesus. . . . The colored people right now are the common people" (*Hedgepeth* 29).

Not only did Allen realize that many, if not most, in his audience were black, but he also realized that they were not well educated. "The revival isn't breaking out among the intellectuals," he once boasted. "The bible says much learning hath made thee mad. So we're making no special effort to reach intellectuals. Jesus didn't" (*Hedge-peth* 29).

In short, those to whom Allen preached belonged to the down scale of society—the poor, the undereducated, the social minorities, but especially the physically afflicted. These latter ones seemed most re-ceptive to his message of healing and deliverance, and it was to these people that he went to great lengths to persuade. Continually offering a measure of hope Allen would plead, "Why should you stay there in a wheelchair? Why should you hobble around on that cane or those crutches? Why should you be blind or partially deaf? Why should you die of cancer, goiter, high blood pressure, disease, sickness, and infirmity? Why should your child there lay on that hot fevered bed when Jesus can heal your body?" "Any sinner can come and be saved and healed at the same time," Allen concluded ("It Is Finished"). From the looks of thousands who flocked to his crusades, he was successful at inducing people to believe him.

ALLEN'S AWARENESS OF THE NEED TO PROVE

A. A. Allen was well aware that many people were skeptical of the miraculous healings. Therefore he went to great lengths not only to bolster the true believers in his audiences but to convince the skeptics themselves that God was operating in the supernatural in his crusades.

Once Allen told of a time when he checked into a hotel in Los Angeles. The desk clerk immediately recognized Allen from the television programs he had seen of him. Regarding the healings that he had seen Allen perform on TV, the desk clerk skeptically asked, "Is that actually real? Are those people actually getting healed?" Allen suggested to his audience that this desk clerk is only one in many who are skeptical. Allen believed that such skepticism is caused by demons and is "a disease of the soul" ("Skepticism").

Once, prior to beginning a healing line, Allen, mimicking an inquisitive audience member, raised the question, "How do you know [that people are healed]?" "Is there any power in your hands to heal the sick?" ("Two Services Under the Tent"). Allen proceeded to answer these questions.

Allen would eventually write in his autobiography that even among preachers and church goers, "Healing is no longer believed despite all the evidence in Scripture that God can, will and does heal the faithful" (Allen and Wagner 162). The point is that Allen was acutely aware that there were unbelievers in his audiences, and he constantly tried to preempt such disbelief wherever and whenever he could. But how? How did Allen attempt to diffuse the "broadsides leveled against me from pulpits, from spokesmen of organized religion, from the press?" (Allen and Wagner 162). A look at his rhetoric shows that his techniques were like other healers of the twentieth century.

REPUDIATION OF PERSONAL POWER

As if taking a lesson from McPherson, Branham, or Roberts, Allen frequently reminded his audiences that God, not he, was the healer. "I'm not a healer, but I'm a believer," retorted Allen in answering how one can be sure that healings occur ("Two Services Under the

Tent"). Once he responded, "I'm not a healer. I couldn't heal any-body" ("This Gospel of the Kingdom"). On another occasion, after laying hands on a woman with Addison's disease, Allen quickly reminded his onlookers, "Listen friends. We are not a healer, but the healer is here" ("Skepticism"). Before healing a man brought to him on a stretcher, Allen quickly reminded the crowd, "I'm not a healer, but tonight I claim power to stand over the devil" (*Miracles Today*). Time and time again Allen made sure that audiences understood that it was not he but God who was performing the miracle. Ostensibly Allen was merely the vessel through whom God chose to operate. This he certainly wanted his audiences to understand and reiterated it often to those who attended his crusades.

As has been mentioned earlier, by giving God the credit, Allen avoided the risk of looking egotistical. This would bolster his credibility as a true man of God, since men of God are supposed to be humble. Lewis reinforces this point when he suggests that if a man like Allen could perform miracles yet still remain humble, then his followers would feel compelled to revere him (184–85). Further, by giving God the credit, this freed Allen from critics if and when a healing failed. Allen could always respond that he had never claimed any power to heal anybody in the first place. Allen preached that before healing could occur, the faith of three personalities must converge in a triangle: (1) the person being prayed for needed faith; (2) Allen needed faith (which he assured his audiences he had); and (3) "God forms the third end of the triangle" ("Two Services Under the Tent"). If a person were not healed, it obviously resulted from a lack of faith on the part of the person seeking the healing because both God and Allen had done their parts.

The fact that someone may not have been healed never daunted Allen. He boasted that "If I laid my hands on a hundred people and ever [sic] one of them had dropped dead while I prayed for 'em, I'd say, 'Bring on a hundred and one.' I'm going to do it again 'cause Jesus told me to" ("This Gospel of the Kingdom"). Allen reminded his audience that even Jesus himself did not raise all of the dead or heal all of the sick. "Where there was no faith, Jesus could do no mighty work," explained Allen ("Allen Exhorting").

ALLEN'S APPEAL TO THE SCRIPTURES

Allen believed that one of the strongest proofs for miraculous healing was found in scripture. Relying on the Bible appeared to be one of the primary ways he induced people to believe. On one occasion, almost out of frustration, Allen demanded, "Listen to me. I am giving you biblical, scriptural proof that in this day and in this hour God declared, and God can't lie. He said, 'I will work a work in your day that you will not believe though it be told you'" ("Skepticism").

One of Allen's favorite passages, which he quoted regularly was Mark 16:17—"These signs shall follow them that believe. They shall lay hands on the sick and they shall recover" ("This Gospel of the Kingdom"). In fact a portion of this verse was printed on a long banner that hung behind Allen's stage in his revival tent to remind audiences that God operates in the miraculous.

Like other faith healers of the twentieth century, Allen was fond of Hebrews 13:8, "Jesus Christ, the same yesterday, and today, and forever." Often Allen would begin his preaching by asking, "Everybody happy tonight? Say amen if you believe everything in God's word. He's the same yesterday, today, and forever. Do you believe everything from Genesis to Revelation? Do you believe everything here?" (*Miracles Today*).

Another favorite passage of Allen was I Peter 2:24, which suggests in part, "by whose stripes ye were healed." During one sermon, for example, Allen read this verse at the top of his voice, pausing between each word. He then punctuated the verse with a loud hand clap to underscore the finality of his point. He was emphatic that this verse proved beyond the shadow of a doubt that miraculous healing was available to anyone who became a Christian ("Allen Exhorting").

Once after reading Matthew 8:17, which suggests in part, "Himself [Jesus] took our infirmities, and bare our sicknesses," Allen offered this verse as proof for healing. "It is salvation for the soul and, thank God, it is also healing for the body" ("Allen Exhorting"). In summary, Allen believed that all scripture is inspired by God and that it is "profitable for doctrine, correction, instruction in the word of righteousness that the man of God may be perfect and entire wanting nothing [II Tim. 3:16]." "How many here believe every bit of God's word?" asked Allen. "Do you believe it from Genesis to Revelation? Do you believe it's God's holy word? That every bit of it is inspired? That it comes straight from heaven?" ("Skepticism"). To Allen, if people believed in God and in the Bible as the word of God, then they must also believe in miraculous healings. In Allen's mind the three were inseparable.

ALLEN'S USE OF TESTIMONIES

When not offering Biblical texts in an attempt to persuade, Allen would use testimonies of those who had received healing to induce cooperation. For example, Allen healed a man who had ruptures of the abdomen and was "deaf in both ears." "This man was so deaf a moment ago he couldn't hear what I said to him. God opened his ears," Allen claimed. Then Allen allowed the man to testify to the audience. "That's right," said the man, "And he's completely healed my body. I don't feel no pain at all" ("Two Services Under the Tent").

Perhaps one of Allen's most sensational testimonies came from an undertaker whose daughter was "healed." At the start of the service Allen informed the audience that he prayed the undertaker's daughter "back from the dead," a rather ambiguous expression in the first place. Half way through the service Allen called the woman's father, Julian B. Hawkins, to the microphone to give his testimony. While Hawkins was making his way to the stage Allen reminded the audience that if anybody knew death when he saw it, an undertaker did. After Allen asked the undertaker if he really believed his daughter was dying, the undertaker testified, "I know it." Informing the audience that he had been an undertaker for thirty years, he said, "she had all the signs of death." He went on to proclaim that had he not made the trip to an A. A. Allen revival on behalf of his daughter, she "would be in the grave now." He explained how, when he visited her the next morning, she was sitting up in the hospital bed reading a newspaper. Allen then introduced the girl and invited her to come forward and sing "How Great Thou Art" to the audience ("Allen Exhorting").

What is interesting about this story is the vague language that both Allen and the undertaker employed. One has to listen closely to exactly what they said. Although in 1965 Allen did claim to be able to raise the dead (Lewis 169, 192), during this crusade neither he nor the undertaker explicitly said that the girl had already died. Instead, they suggested that she was only near death, perhaps very sick, but not yet deceased. Phrases such as "back from the dead" and "was dying" suggested only that the girl was very sick. Many listening, however, probably did not understand this and believed that Allen had indeed raised someone from the dead.

In addition to the numerous testimonies that Allen invoked from people in his healing lines, he relied heavily upon testimonies in his monthly periodical *Miracle Magazine*. In fact, with the exception of a few items such as Allen's revival schedules, book advertisements, and radio and television logs, most of *Miracle Magazine* was dedicated to reprinting letters, stories, or personal testimonies of individuals who had written to Allen, claiming a spiritual, physical, or financial healing.

The cover story for the January 1960 edition of *Miracle Magazine*, for example, was entitled "I Took My Cancer to Church in a Jar." The story is told about a Reverend Wilkins, who after becoming sick at a restaurant was taken to an A. A. Allen revival to be healed. While sitting in the back of the tent he fell unconscious. After the ushers carried him to the platform where Allen could pray for him, he "rose from the stretcher a well man—and went running and leaping around the tent." The man returned the next night "with six cancers in a jar, which he had passed since his healing the night before." *Miracle Magazine* reports Wilkins to have said, "I feel fine. God performed the operation!" (Jan. 1960, 1 and 7).

Other testimonies involved sensational claims such as seeing demon-possessed people set free, receiving "new lungs," being cured of hemophilia, growing an arm six inches longer, or passing an open safety pin from the stomach up the esophagus through the mouth (*Miracle Magazine* Oct. 1959, 12; Dec. 1959, 11; Jan. 1960, 3–5). One woman even claimed that God miraculously filled a decayed tooth with gold (*Miracle Magazine* Oct. 1961, 5; Lewis 194).

Often these sensational stories were accompanied by pictures of the cured as if they were telling their own story in front of a live audience. In addition to pictures of individuals, it was common to see photographs of "over-capacity crowds" in attendance at an A. A. Allen revival (*Miracle Magazine* Oct. 1959, 9). No doubt, these pictures were designed to persuade the reader that wonderful things were happening to thousands of people who believed in what A. A. Allen was doing. Captions surrounding some of these pictures made Allen crusades sound exciting: "A Salvation Altar Call," "Double Portion Night," "Mass Miracle Night," "Slain Under the Power of God," and "Ordination Night." These pictures appealed to one's interpersonal inclusion needs. They showed what an individual was missing by not being in attendance at these revivals. Ultimately, they served to convince people that they, too, could receive a miracle and that, they too, should attend Allen's revivals. (*Miracle Magazine* Dec. 1959, 9). After all, anybody who was anybody spiritually thronged to the Allen crusades. Why sit at home and miss out on the excitement?

Testimony is a powerful device to induce belief in others and Allen understood this. Rhetorical theorist William Norwood Brigance points out that "Often listeners will not take [the speaker's] unsupported word, but will respect the judgment of others" (109–110). Likewise, McBurney and Wrage, contemporary rhetorical theorists of Allen, point out that "personal testimony" is one of the "most effective means of elaborating the points of your speech" (327–29). Obviously, Allen sensed this and employed testimony freely, whether in print or by word of mouth in front of large audiences. There can be no doubt that it worked to convince many.

In addition to personal testimony from those who had received miraculous healings, Allen occasionally relied upon the testimony of experts. This is most easily seen in his autobiography where Allen relied, ironically enough, on intellectuals. After castigating the *Greensboro Record* for what Allen felt was a slap at his ministry, he praised it for consulting respected authorities about the nature of worship at Allen's revivals. Allen reproduced the testimonies of Dr. J. Floyd Moore, a Guilford College professor, Reverend Julius T. Douglas of St. James Presbyterian Church, and Reverend William Currie of the First Presbyterian Church to give legitimacy to Allen's ministry. Even though Allen was quoting the *Greensboro Record*, in doing so, he was associating his deeds with respected ministers and theologians (not to mention the newspaper itself) in an attempt to legitimize his actions (Allen and Wagner 172). Rhetorical theorists McBurney and Wrage point out that "the opinion of an expert has claims to credibility which we cannot extend to the opinion of a layman" (138). Allen apparently understood this and used it to his advantage.

Allen also made mention of the intelligentsia directly associated with his ministry. "My critics would be surprised at the number of brilliant, college-trained men and women who worship at my revivals . . . and preach in our world-wide ministry," he once explained. While these people were in the minority, which Allen immediately recognized, they were there nonetheless, and Allen used them to his credit whenever it was to his advantage (Allen and Wagner 164).

Like other faith healers in our study, Allen was not content to rely solely on testimonies of those who were healed or experts in the field. He occasionally offered testimony about his own life. In fact Allen's entire life was a testimonial, given the fact that he had such an immoral past. Lewis suggests that Allen loved to retell "the sordid story of his childhood" because it proved that God was able to save even the vilest of sinners (163). That is, if God could save A. A. Allen, he could save anyone. If this were the case, then Allen would be vindicated in front of his audiences.

Not only did Allen retell how merciful God was to him spiritually, but he also retold how he had received his own personal healing. He disclosed, for example, how he lost his voice while straining to preach night after night during World War II. Eventually he developed "tightness and harshness" in his voice and was "barely able to whisper." In Indianapolis one night he had to apologize to the audience for not being able to preach and walked away from the podium, dejected. The doctors told him that his vocal cords were permanently damaged and that he would never preach again. He was told to find a job that did not involve talking and move to Arizona which has a dry climate. But Allen could not accept the verdict of three doctors. He recounted how he realized that he had God on his side so he asked a friend, who happened to be a pastor, to lay hands on him and cast out the demon of fear that was gripping him.

Allen tells how, as his friend prayed, he felt a "fluttering" inside his stomach. He felt the demons leave him. He felt unburdened and joyous. He then realized that the loud shouts that he heard were coming from his own voice. "My 'ruined' vocal cords were as good as new." Allen claims that he wanted to revisit all of his doctors to show them what the power of God had accomplished in him, that what was beyond medicine was "a trifle to the Lord" (Allen and Wagner 118). Clearly, such personal narratives are persuasive tactics to employ to convince Allen's constituency that God can heal them just as He healed Allen. This is just one more example of how Allen appeared to have understood the power of testimony.

ALLEN'S APPEAL TO ONE'S EYES

Like many other faith healers in the twentieth century, to Allen seeing was believing. When he told his audience about the skepticism of the hotel clerk in Los Angeles he turned to the camera and reminded his viewers that what they saw was actually what happened.

"The camera picks them [miracles] up just as they happen. Actually, it's a part of the service." Then, turning his back to the audience and addressing the guest ministers who were sitting on stage with him, he reminded them, "You preachers everyone of you know what we televise here in these healing lines . . . it has not happened before. People we've never seen before, people I've never met before. They come into the . . . service and we pray for them as they come on the ramp" ("Skepticism").

Allen loved nothing more than to demonstrate empirically to an audience how an individual had been healed. Not only was this approach compelling to an audience, but it was also entertaining. Whether it was taking sick people by the hand and raising them from a stretcher or asking a deaf person who had been healed to repeat "Thank you, Jesus," "Praise the Lord," "Hallelujah" or some other simplistic, easily recalled expression, Allen always made sure that individuals demonstrated their new-found health to the audience ("Allen Exhorting"). Once, after healing an individual with a bad back, Allen jumped into his arms and asked him to pick him up after he had the man bend over and touch his toes several times for the audience to witness ("It is Finished"). On another occasion, after healing a man with "big knots" all over his back, Allen had the man lift a carrying case of TV equipment to demonstrate the healing for the audience. Immediately afterward Allen sat a little girl on the platform beside him and pulled her shorter right leg even with her left for the audience to see. The crowd cheered as they watched the little girl run back to her seat. Allen proceeded to ask the audience if they believed God had "done something for her" ("This Gospel of the Kingdom").

One of Allen's most entertaining cases on television involved a man who had been raised from a stretcher. Allen allowed the man to eat his lunch while sitting on stage with him to show the audience that the man had fully recovered from stomach cancer. "Did you bring your dinner?" Allen asked the man. Allen then commanded his assistants to bring the man a carton of milk and a ham salad sandwich. Then Allen laid his hands on the man's stomach, cursed the cancer, and yelled, "Brother, in the name of Jesus, I command you, Get up!" Much to the delight of the audience, the man arose from the stretcher. Allen then handed the man a one-quart carton of milk, placed his hands on the man's stomach, and said, "I command it to go down." As the man turned the carton up and began drinking, Allen felt the carton and assured the audience, "It's just goin' clear down." When the man finished drinking, Allen turned the carton upside down to show the audience that there was no more milk in it. He then unwrapped the sandwich and handed it to the man who proceeded to eat. After being asked how he felt, the man responded that he felt fine. (*Miracles Today*).

As was the case with most of Allen's healings, no one really knew to what extent the man was sick. Audiences just saw a man arise from a stretcher after having Allen lay his hands on him and command the sickness to come out of him. This was enough, though, as gasps of astonishment and shouts of "Thank you, Jesus" or "Praise the Lord" arose from the audience. Allen certainly understood what he was doing, though, whenever he attempted to demonstrate empirically that a healing had taken place. He knew that if he could show how God had healed a person, then he could convince them that they could be healed and that Allen was God's chosen vessel.

Beside healings Allen testified how other empirical events occurred in his revivals that served to convince his audiences that he was sent from God. For example, he recounts how during one revival, a twenty-foot flame of fire appeared over his tent in the night sky. During the same meeting miracle oil appeared on the hands of many in attendance. Allen's cameraman R. E. Kemery supposedly recorded the events on film. Also during that meeting Allen tells of how a cross of blood appeared on his forehead as a sign that God had called him and was validating his ministry. The multitudes who saw it, suggested Allen, were "living witnesses to the sign God placed on me" (Allen and Wagner 141–44; see also *Miracle Magazine* Jan. 1956, 2). Obviously Allen told these stories in an attempt to prove to people that the miraculous commonly occurred in his revivals.

ALLEN'S SERMON ORGANIZATION

Rhetorical theorists Brigance and Immel point out that good organization facilitates an audience's learning, edification, and retention (294–95). While Allen's repudiation of personal claims, use of scriptures and testimonies, and reliance on empirical proof often sold the idea of the miraculous to his followers, the format in which he presented them contributed little if anything. In a word, Allen's sermons were nothing short of desultory.

During Allen's crusades, after a toe-tapping song or two, R. W.

Shambach would introduce him: "At this time it's my very happy pleasure and privilege to present to this audience the man that God has mightily anointed with a miracle ministry, God's man of faith and power, Reverend A. A. Allen." Allen would then bound in front of the audience and begin by shouting something like, "If you believe everything in this book, say amen." Then he would read a passage from the Bible and proceed to talk about it in a rambling fashion. There were never discernible main points that supported a thesis as in the preaching of Oral Roberts. Moreover, as Lewis notes, Allen generally preached no longer than fifteen or twenty minutes at the most (174).

Often Allen's sermons revolved around entire individuals who were present before the audience. Once, for example, after beginning his sermon by reading Malachi 3:9 and Deuteronomy 28:14–16, Allen called forth a lady from the audience who had brought with her a six-year-old, deformed boy whose arms and legs resembled that of a monkey. Holding the little boy in his arms throughout much of his preaching Allen proceeded to explain that God had cursed the baby at birth for the sins of his parents. He warned people in the audience that if they did not want to have children born like this, "you'd better raise your hands to heaven and say, 'My God, I'll serve you.' " Over and over again he pleaded with people to "flee from your sins" ("Monkey Boy"). No discernible main points, however, were offered in support of a thesis. This type of sensationalism was typical of Allen. Ironically, Allen's lack of organization did not appear to impede his rhetorical progress, perhaps because his audience was not expecting an orderly discussion of ideas in the first place and because he was so dynamic and entertaining to watch. Organization, therefore, became a non-entity in Allen's attempts to persuade others.

ALLEN'S STYLE AND DELIVERY

Of all the elements that made A. A. Allen a successful faith healer, one of the strongest would have been the way he delivered his messages to his audiences, whether while preaching or healing. Allen was a consummate showman. Entertainment was central to his ministry. In fact, Allen himself, once made the remark that he could not remember a time in his life when it did not seem natural for him to dance and sing. Since music and rhythm were early influences in his life, his "first ambition" was to be a singer, a musician, an entertainer, or an actor (Allen and Wagner 43–44). Although Allen never made it to Hollywood, he often entertained revival audiences with his singing, preaching, and healing.

After occasionally singing an opening song Allen would begin to preach. He never spoke from an outline or prepared notes which allowed him maximum eye contact and interaction with his audience. He almost always spoke in a loud, personable voice. Often his words rolled off his tongue in rapid-fire succession. Morris suggests that Allen's "raspy, rapid-fire Ozark baritone voice gave his sermons a distinctive flavor" (12). Constantly in motion he paced about, gesturing wildly with both hands as he held his Bible in his right hand ("Monkey Boy"). Once when preaching, as he walked approximately ten to fifteen feet away from his small white podium on the platform, he shouted at the top of his lungs, "You shall receive power after the Holy Ghost has come upon you." He then returned to the podium and smacked it forcefully with his right hand. Then he raised his hand making a karate-chopping motion in front of his bent-over body as he yelled to his audience, "If there was ever a time men and women in the world tonight need the baptism of the Holy Ghost and the power that comes with it, it's now!" ("Power"). Lewis suggests, "Seldom appearing out of breath, the energetic Allen was a non-stop bundle of energy once he mounted the speaking platform" (198). Morris concurs when he offers, "With a microphone in his hand and his coat discarded, he prowled the platform like a caged tiger, his visage as fierce as that of an Old Testament prophet. . . . He tried to preach the devil out of every congregation he faced" (12).

After a sermon which, as noted earlier lasted only about fifteen to twenty minutes, Allen began receiving people in the healing line. Here he was equally adept at entertaining an audience with his non-verbal mannerisms. When healing individuals Allen would often bounce on his toes in pogo-stick fashion while making a chopping motion with his right hand behind his head ("This Gospel of the Kingdom"; *Miracles Today*). While Allen could gently lay his hands on some poor soul seeking a miracle, more often than not, he was inclined to clasp both hands firmly around an individual's head or place his index fingers squarely in their ears and ring them around in circles while crying for the demons of deafness to come out or the demons of some other disease to leave them. In short, Allen was animated. His dynamism—whether while preaching or healing the sick—was immediately apparent and it was such dynamism that contributed to his persuasive success.

CONCLUSION

Doubtless, A. A. Allen was one of the most popular faith healers in America in the years following World War II. His popularity continued well into the 1960s. Like Branham, it is likely that Allen's popularity would have rivaled that of Oral Roberts had he lived as long as Roberts has. Perhaps like Roberts, Allen's name would have been a household word.

While there are indeed differences between A. A. Allen and the other healers we have looked at thus far in this study (e.g., Allen's early immoral lifestyle), there are probably more striking parallels. Like Branham and Roberts, Allen was reared in back-breaking poverty. Like Branham, yet for different reasons, Allen ran into trouble with civil authorities. Like McPherson, Branham, and Roberts, Allen relied on similar rhetorical appeals. He disavowed personal ability to heal, appearing as a humble servant of God. He leaned heavily on personal and secondary testimony. He employed scriptures. He depended, in part, on empirical proofs. All of these proofs convinced followers that they too could receive what Allen and thousands of others after him had received—a personal miracle. And what's more, with perhaps the exception of preaching more to blacks than any of the other healers, Allen preached to the same kinds of audiences as did McPherson, Branham, and Roberts. They were poor, underprivileged, and physically and mentally frail who sought relief from life's hardships. And like McPherson, Branham, and Roberts, Allen too, knew how to persuade them.

Allen will long be remembered as a controversial figure. History will not allow us to forget his drunk driving charge and subsequent excommunication by the Assemblies of God. And so there will always be those who view him as an alcoholic con man. But for many, for whatever reasons known only to them, such actions did not significantly detract from Allen's image as God's vessel of healing. To them, A. A. Allen will forever be revered. He will always be known as "God's man of faith and power."

REFERENCES

Allen, Asa Alonzo, and Walter Wagner. *Born to Lose, Bound to Win: An Autobiography.* Garden City, NY: Doubleday & Co., 1970.

"Allen Exhorting." *Miracles Today* (Television Program). n.d. Holy Spirit Research Center. Oral Roberts University.

Brigance, William Norwood. *Speech Communication.* 2nd ed. New York: Appleton-Century-Crofts, 1955.

Brigance, William Norwood, and Ray Keeslar Immel. *Speechmaking: Principles and Practice.* New York: Crofts, 1947.

"Faith Healers: Getting Back Double From God." *Time* 7 March 1969: 64–65.

Hanegraaff, Hendrik H. "What's Wrong with The Faith Movement—Part One: E. W. Kenyon and the Twelve Apostles of Another Gospel." *Christian Research Journal* (Winter 1993): 16. Christian Research Institute, 1994. http://icinet93.icinet.

Harrell, David E., Jr. *All Things Are Possible: The Healing and Charismatic Revivals in Modern America.* Bloomington, IN: Indiana University Press, 1975.

Hedgepeth, William. *Look* 7 Oct. 1969: 23–31.

"It is Finished." *Miracles Today* (Television Program). n.d. Holy Spirit Research Center. Oral Roberts University.

Lewis, Todd Vernon. "Charismatic Communication and Faith Healers: A Critical Study of Rhetorical Behavior." Diss. Louisiana State University, 1980.

McBurney, James H., and Ernest J. Wrage. *The Art of Good Speech.* New York: Prentice-Hall, 1953.

Melton, J. Gordon, Phillip Charles Lucas, and Jon R. Stone. *Prime-Time Religion: An Encyclopedia of Religious Broadcasting.* Phoenix, AZ: Oryx Press, 1997.

Miracle Magazine. Jan. 1956.

Miracle Magazine. Oct. 1959.

Miracle Magazine. Dec. 1959.

Miracle Magazine. Jan. 1960.

Miracle Magazine. Oct. 1961.

Miracles Today (Television Program). No program title. n.d. Holy Spirit Research Center. Oral Roberts University.

"Monkey Boy." *Miracles Today* (Television Program). n.d. Holy Spirit Research Center. Oral Roberts University.

Morris, James. *The Preachers.* New York: St. Martin's Press, 1973.

"Power." *Miracles Today* (Television Program). n.d. Holy Spirit Research Center. Oral Roberts University.

"Reverend A. A. Allen, Evangelist, Dies." *New York Times* 14 June 1970: 93.

Simson, Eve. *The Faith Healer: Deliverance Evangelism in North America*. New York: Pyramid Books, 1977.

"Skepticism." *Miracles Today* (Television Program). n.d. Holy Spirit Research Center. Oral Roberts University.

Stewart, Don. *The Man from Miracle Valley*. Long Beach, CA: Great Horizons Co., 1971.

"This Gospel of the Kingdom Shall Be Preached in All The World." *The Allen Revival Hour* (Television Program). n.d. Holy Spirit Research Center. Oral Roberts University.

This is Miracle Valley Video. n.d. Holy Spirit Research Center. Oral Roberts University.

"Two Services Under the Tent." *The Allen Revival Hour* (Television Program). n.d. Holy Spirit Research Center. Oral Roberts University.

CHAPTER FIVE

Akron's Idiosyncratic Evangelist and Faith Healer: Ernest Angley

The year was 1988. On this cold, rainy Friday evening in February, just as on other Friday nights, they came in droves. Some craved spiritual nourishment. Others sought a physical healing. But whatever their need, people of all ages scurried excitedly into the 3,000 seat auditorium of Grace Cathedral on South Canton Road in Akron, Ohio. There Ernest Angley, dynamic minister and founder of the non-denominational church, carefully orchestrated his weekly miracle service, something he had been doing for decades.

Upon entering Grace Cathedral one would immediately be awed by the ornate surroundings. A female organist played softly as a few individuals mourning over sins or other personal struggles intermittently arose and walked listlessly to the altar to pray. The mood was somber, much like that of a death parlor. In fact, with its blue velvet curtains trimmed in gold fringe and tassels and its blue and red carpet that turned purple when viewed from an angle, the quiet auditorium gave the impression of a funeral home. The solemn ambiance was occasionally broken by ushers clad in black suits and bow ties straightening electric cords, carrying pitchers of water, or greeting visitors.

Around seven o'clock the choir, bedecked in robes, began filing onto the stage as the organ continued to play softly. Shortly the show

Ernest Angley, July 24, 1984. Courtesy of the *[Akron] Beacon Journal*. Photographer: Paul Tople. Reprinted with permission.

would begin. The solemn mood would soon give way to rafter-raising singing, shouting, and applauding. After her opening remarks, extolling the virtues of Jesus and reminding the audience how wonderful it is to be a Christian, the female choir director led the congregation in singing "Have Thine Own Way Lord." Then the choir sang a couple of fast-paced songs, both of which brought a round of applause from the audience. As another woman from the choir stepped to the microphone to encourage people to donate to Ernest Angley's various projects, ten ushers carrying bags for the contributions lined the front of the auditorium in a state of readiness to collect money from the five sections of pews. After the contributions were completed and the choir filed out one by one as the piano played "We Will Follow the Steps of Jesus," the audience settled in for an even bigger thrill.

Suddenly a man appeared at the microphone to introduce the person everyone had come to see. After a few comments, like a circus announcer, he enthusiastically barked, "And now it gives me great pleasure to introduce to you the Reverend Ernest Angley." With excitement in the air, a short, portly figure wearing a toupee and carrying a Bible with 8 ½-by-11-inch papers protruding from it strolled onto the stage, grinning from ear to ear. Upon laying his notes on the podium he hopped out of the pulpit and into the audience. Quickly moving in front of each of the five sections of pews, as if he were leading cheers, Angley repeatedly yelled, "Hallelujah!" or "Amen!" Each section then enthusiastically responded with the same word. Then he briskly walked back into the pulpit to continue working up the audience.

It was obvious that the crowd knew exactly what to say and do. Angley frequently began a sentence but intentionally failed to complete it so that those in attendance could supply the missing word. For instance, he asked, "You're a what?" The audience yelled in unison, "A winner!" Then, he asked, "With God, all things are . . . ?" "Possible!" responded the enthusiastic crowd as they supplied the correct reply. With the audience now more excited than ever, Angley proceeded to ask for money for his television ministry. "I want all those who are going to give one hundred dollars to wave at God," begged Angley. After a brief pause he lowered the amount: "All those who are going to give fifty dollars, wave at God." "Twenty-five dollars, twenty"—like Abraham bargaining with God over the city of Sodom—gradually Angley asked that each of these donors wave at God. Then, dropping the amount to ten, five, three, two, and one,

Angley asked that these contributors stand up. By this point he had even asked for pocket change. Gradually people began filing to the front to hand Angley their offering. As he eagerly looked on the outside of every envelope to see how much money each person was giving, Angley responded, "Thank You," or "God Bless You."

After he solicited his audience for money some two or three times for one project or another, Angley began a desultory sermon that lasted for nearly an hour. Then came the part in his service in which Angley invited those who had come for the first time, who had traveled a long distance, or who had come from another state to form a line so that he might lay his hands on them to be healed. "Come right on. Whatever it is, God will heal." One by one, as people crowded to the stage, Angley laid his hands on those who reportedly had tumors on their lungs, lumps in their breasts, suicidal tendencies and other emotional problems, inner ear trouble, and smoking and drinking habits, to name a few. "Wilt thou be made whole?" Angley frequently asked a willing subject. "Loose her in the name of the Lord," he screamed. Then he admonished the individual, "Go and get well." Angley also shouted, "Heeeyul! Heeeyul! Heeeeeeeyul! dear Jesus," in which case the audience erupted in applause (Observation by the author).

For anyone attending one of these Friday evening performances, it was clear that Angley was popular among his followers. This night Angley boasted, "We've had as high as fifteen countries and twenty-eight states just in one service. And they come from all over." Once he proudly proclaimed that one woman even "flew in from Russia to get her miracle and had to go back" (Interview by Griffith). Visiting one of these services himself prompted James Randi to write in his book *The Faith Healers* that to his parishioners, Angley is a God-inspired preacher. "We found that most of those in attendance at the church were accustomed to being there every Friday night. It was their night out in very much the way other folks go to the drive-in movie or the bowling alley once a week" (238).

In addition to his Friday night followers Angley has also amassed a large gathering of television viewers. While he is not as well known as some televangelists, he is, nonetheless, a national figure at one time appearing in approximately twenty-nine markets with 37,000 households watching him each week (Arbitron). According to Angley himself, at one point he was reaching into 139 countries, had a total television audience of over one million for the month of January

1988, and was viewed by 358,000 households during the week of February 7, 1988 (Observation by the author). Angley's own organization reports that *Stern* magazine, billed as one of the largest in Europe, once referred to him as the United States' "super star of religion" and that the American people consider him to be "the most gifted TV preacher in the land" (Angley, *Cell 15* xiv–xv). While this description is clearly sensationalized by Angley's organization, there can be no doubt that thousands of people revere him.

ANGLEY'S BACKGROUND

Ernest Angley was born into a Baptist family in Mooresville, North Carolina approximately thirty miles north of Charlotte in 1922. One of seven children whose father was a poor textile worker, Angley spent two years at Lee College in Cleveland, Tennessee "mostly on faith." "I didn't have any money," he explains. While in school there, he met his future wife Esther Lee Sikes, the daughter of Mr. and Mrs. William N. Sikes. Sikes was "a railroad man" from Wimauma, Florida where Esther was born (de Groot G-4; " 'Angel' of Grace Cathedral Dies" n.p.). According to a biographical sketch of Angley provided by his organization, he and Esther were married in November 1943, the same year Angley was licensed to preach.

Newspaper accounts reveal that Angley began part-time preaching shortly after his conversion at age eighteen. Prior to coming to Akron, he and "Angel," as he affectionately called his wife, traveled around the United States and the Caribbean for more than ten years holding revivals in auditoriums and tents. "Angel" played the organ and her husband preached.

In June 1954 they rolled into Akron with two semi-trailers, a large tent, and an air-conditioned house trailer. The tent was erected on a hill near the present site of Grace Cathedral and was called the Temple of Healing Stripes, a name inspired by Isaiah 53:5. When it was dismantled for the winter, Angley moved the congregation that he had attracted into the Old Liberty Theatre on West Market Street in downtown Akron. There they met until the spring of 1955 when they built a wooden-frame structure on twenty acres of land on Canton Road in southeast Akron. Before purchasing this land, some accounts suggest Angley waved a pocket-size Bible over it, which he carried with him on business deals to signify he was claiming it for the Lord. The newly erected wooden building, also known as the

Temple of Healing Stripes, was constructed through volunteer labor and offerings. In 1957 work began on a newer, larger building costing 1.3 million dollars to accommodate a 3,000 member congregation. It was completed in April 1958 and was given the name Grace Cathedral (de Groot G-4; Haferd, personal interview; Interview by Griffith). In the early 1990s Angley purchased Rex Hubbard's old building off State Road in Akron, known as the Cathedral of Tomorrow. After changing its name to "Ernest Angley's Grace Cathedral," which is plastered across the front of the building, Angley moved his seat of operations there. The old Grace Cathedral is currently used as a school.

HEALINGS THROUGH GOD'S POWER BUT A PERSON'S FAITH

Ernest Angley clearly qualifies as a faith healer. And he is one of the most popular ones in America today. He is probably best known for laying his hands on an individual and yelling, "Thou foul, deaf spirits, come out!" "Ya-eee! Come out of him thou foul demons," or some similar expression ("The Ninety and Nine Club" 1997).

Although he claims to be endowed with a special gift for bringing deliverance to the sick, he frequently makes it clear to his audience that it is God who does the healing, not himself (Angley, *Confidence* 24). Sounding like all other faith healers in this study, he suggests, "Friend, man is a flimsy substitute for God. We must, above all, look to our God. Remember, man cannot heal; God is the healer." Angley frequently advertises, "Absolutely all of the credit and honor for healing is given to God" (Angley, *Faith in God Heals the Sick* 29). Additionally, Angley's organization makes it clear that he does not claim to be a faith healer but merely a "witness of the marvelous healing power of Christ" (Angley *Lukewarm Christians* 24). He frequently remarks to his audiences, "I am not a healer. I do not claim to be" (Observation by the author).

Angley teaches his listeners that faith is a prerequisite to healing. He argues that "nothing can keep you from being healed if you are willing to act whole-heartedly on the Word. There is no room for if's, might's, or hope-so's" (*Faith in God Heals the Sick* 15). Furthermore, he relates how many people come into his healing lines at his crusades and church services shaking with fear because they are worried they do not have sufficient faith to be healed. "If you can look up into the face of God and say, 'Lord, I believe every chapter, every verse, every word,' then you have enough faith to be healed of any affliction or disease." If one does not have faith, however, he or she cannot be healed. Citing Romans 10:17, Angley suggests that a person obtains faith by reading and meditating on the Word of God (*Faith in God Heals the Sick* 36–37, 39).

Angley further contends that even after recovering from a disease one can lose his or her health if that person loses faith in God. "Anything obtained through faith can be lost through doubt. Anything you get from God through obedience can be lost through disobedience." In other words, backsliders can expect to lose their miracle (*Faith in God Heals the Sick* 56).

ANGLEY'S PROOF IS IN THE WORD

Like other faith healers Angley frequently invokes scriptures to support his contention that God heals people supernaturally of their infirmities. One of Angley's favorite passages is Isaiah 53:5 which suggests in part, "With his stripes we are healed." Angley believes that salvation and physical healing are a two-fold atonement. "Because of the Old Rugged Cross, because of a man called Jesus we can reach God directly today for salvation, for healing" (*The Power of the Cross* 17).

In addition Angley draws on Matthew 18:19 to demonstrate the power of prayer in healing. He remarks, "The Bible says in Matthew 18:19, 'That if two of you shall agree on earth as touching any thing that they shall ask, it shall be done for them of my Father which is in heaven.'" Hence, he encourages, "If there is something special you would like me to pray with you about—a special problem or need—write to me and I will pray over your requests" (*The Greatness of the Fire of the Holy Spirit* 25).

Further drawing on the New Testament, Ernest Angley preaches that individuals need a point of contact through which to release their faith. At the close of all of his televised sermons he asks those who are sick at home to place their hands on the television as a point of contact in order to receive their miracle (*The Ernest Angley Hour* Feb. 7 and 21, 1988). He also advertises blessed cloths that his ministry sends to people as a point of contact. "Many have been healed by this method. Read about its use in Acts 19:11–12," he suggests ("Abide in God's Love" 11). To justify this practice and to boost his ethos, Angley explains how individuals in the apostle Paul's day "were healed simply by faith in the cloths Paul had anointed with miracle power. The cloths didn't heal, they were a point of contact people used to release their faith so they could accept miracles" (*The Greatness of the Fire of the Holy Spirit* 16).

In fact practically anything will serve as a point of contact for Angley no matter how bizarre it might sound. For instance, in a letter advertising February 15, 1988 as Mountain Day, Angley suggested to his readers that they tear off the upper left-hand corner of the page and keep it as a special point of contact when "we will pray one for another and ask God to grant each request" (Letter to the author, Feb. 1988). Furthermore, he remarks that in the New Testament aprons, handkerchiefs, oil, the laying on of hands, and even shadows and mud were points of contact for deliverance of the sick. Although points of contact are important and can include almost anything, a person still needs faith to be healed, according to Angley (*Faith in God Heals the Sick* 45; *Cell 15*, addendum, ii). However the miracle comes—whether through prayer or physical points of contact—Angley justifies these practices through references to the Bible.

Essentially, referencing the Bible is the cornerstone of Angley's rhetoric. In other words, he frequently tries to persuade people to believe on the basis of some scriptural reference to what he is teaching. Once while being interviewed, Angley advertised his book *Faith in God Heals the Sick* by noting, "so many have been healed by reading that book." "There's so much Bible in there." In the same interview he attempted to sell his book *The Power of Bible Fasting* by suggesting that there is "plenty of scripture to back it all up." "God made us a promise. His word will endure forever" ("The Ninety and Nine Club"). Angley truly believes that he has a license to preach and practice what he does because he can find it in the Bible—or at least he thinks he can. This approach appears to work with many of his constituencies.

GOD'S CALLING, GOD'S HEALING: ANGLEY'S PERSONAL TESTIMONY

In addition to the above rhetorical appeals, Angley teaches that God occasionally speaks and appears to him. "Visions are not imagination. [T]he objects in them appear as they would in life. God's contacts are definite . . . changing you in a way that is unforgettable."

Angley reveals that his first visitation came when he was only seven, when God showed him millions of stars and told him that this would be the number of souls he would eventually lead to Christ. He recalls, "I was on my bed, my head buried in the pillow, and the bed began to spin around and around until I was out in space under the stars. Stars were everywhere; it was a fantastic experience that lingered with me through the years" (*Untying God's Hands* 129–30)

Angley relates how shortly after his conversion at age eighteen, the Lord appeared to him again to anoint him to preach. "The annointing [sic] of the Lord came upon me and I just started preaching," he recounts. "I had been saved for about five weeks when the preacher in my church asked me to talk. I was going to read a bit from the Scriptures and sit down. That was all." Then, something suddenly happened. According to Angley, "[T]he power of the Lord came into me and I went into a cloud of glory. There was a brilliant light all around me" (de Groot G-4). He recounts how when he first started to preach, "I would be caught up in the glory of the Lord so much that the faces in the audience would seem to swim before my eyes . . ." (*Untying God's Hands* 142).

Angley also tells how in 1945 the Lord came to him one night and healed him of a stomach ulcer. He recalls how the Lord appeared in a blinding light. There Christ told him "that I was to go on a long fast and that He would give me his power of healing others and that I was to carry the ministry of healing to the multitudes." Suggesting that the Lord sometimes appears to him while he is on stage preaching, Angley says, "I can see all of him and he looks very much like many paintings of Jesus" (de Groot G-4).

In 1970, shortly before burying his wife "Angel," Angley relates how God appeared to him again. "Her going was planned even before we were married," he explains. "God knew exactly when He was going to take her. He explained to me a future with no Angel. He showed me that together we had won a multitude of souls; and the rest of the souls . . . would have to be won without her. He also told me that by His taking her when He did, she would bring more souls into His kingdom than had He left her with me" (*Cell 15* 27).

One of his most vividly told visitations from God, however, occurred in a prison cell in Munich, Germany on July 11, 1984. Jailed by the Munich authorities for practicing medicine without a license, among other charges, Angley, after several hours under house arrest in his hotel room, was locked in a narrow cell for eight-and-a-half hours. He recalls, "But in that foul depressing place the Spirit of God was with me; the cell filled with the glory of God. [S]omething special was to happen in that cell. [T]he light of God . . . shone down from heaven on me. [G]od began to sing through me—the same song He had sung through me when I was eighteen. [After singing] in another tongue and then in English I began to go into visions, one after another" (*Cell 15* 40–41).

He relates how the cross of Christ would appear to him "in liquid fire." Then it would appear "in royal blue—miracle power." Sometimes it would appear to be "both the cross of miracle power and healing power." He discloses, "The Lord was just living with me, and I had the strength of many men even after all those hours I'd been up! Every part of me was anointed, my bones, my flesh" (*Cell 15* 40–41).

But the Lord apparently was not through speaking to Angley in Munich. On July 12, a hail storm rained down on the city causing extensive damage to buildings, automobiles, and airplanes. He relates how God told him that this was going to occur as punishment for his imprisonment. "God got us out of there, and then He rained judgment just like He promised. God said He sent it, and He'd take full credit" (*Cell 15* 54, 57, 60).

After the Munich incident Angley discloses that God appeared to him again telling him to sue the city. "Although I told people right after my release that I didn't think I would sue, when God let me know He wanted the lawsuits, I moved on it. Man may say 'forgive,' but God sent judgment. God meant business; God told me to sue. [W]ho am I to withstand God?" asks Angley (*Cell 15* 60). Eventually the Munich incident ended in Angley's paying 25,000 marks of his 40,000 mark bond to the city of Munich and 5,000 marks to the Salvation Army of Munich—the charity of Angley's choice (Haferd "The Faith Healing Arrest That Did Wonders" B4).

Angley tells his stories about seeing visions and being called by God so vividly and confidently that it becomes difficult, if not impossible, for his blue-collar, Bible-believing audience to reject his claims. And, "if God has called the Reverend Angley," goes the reasoning, "who am I not to believe in him?"

ANGLEY'S HUMILITY AND SINCERITY

Probably one of Ernest Angley's most attractive features is his humility. As was noted earlier, prior to the beginning of his healing services, Angley usually disclaims having any power to perform healings. Therefore, whenever he suggests, "Thou knowest, oh God, that I never take any of the honor. I never claim any of the glory. I am just a weakness to your greatness," his audience perceives him to be humble, and therefore credible as an evangelist (Observation by the author).

Once when asked by Cleveland television personality Fred Griffith if he tailored his messages to his various constituencies, Angley responded, "No! No! No! I carry the message of Jesus. This is the Jesus ministry. And everything is centered around Jesus, not around Ernest Angley. God forbid. Jesus is the one." Angley emphatically asserted, "I'm not trying to build Ernest Angley. I'm working on building His [Christ's] kingdom" (Interview by Griffith). Eugene White suggests that with "increased confidence acquired by successful experience," speakers often "develop exalted opinions of themselves." White also suggests that when such conceit is noticed by one's audience, it irritates them. "Modesty, is an indispensable asset in interpersonal relations," he advises. Therefore, he warns speakers against "parading" their accomplishments before their audiences (215). Apparently, Ernest Angley recognizes this and strives to convey his modesty to his hearers, lest they become disillusioned with his success.

In addition to his humility Angley also consciously expresses sincerity about what he is doing. Even James Randi in his stinging attack on faith healers admits this much (239). When asked by Fred Griffith why he uses high-tech communication equipment such as television, cable, and satellite dishes to disseminate his message, Angley responded, "I'm a born evangelist. And I evangelize people. And I have this message burning in my heart. And I want to tell everybody." In the same interview Angley disclosed how he never had much money as a boy. This, he assured those watching, "conditioned me and prepared me for the ministry. When I think of money, I think of helping people. I think of souls, and I love to feed the starving, clothe the naked. I love to let them know that Jesus loves them" (Interview by Griffith).

Even in his healing lines Angley exudes the image of a sincere man of God. In the Friday night service attended by this author, for example, when a couple brought their three-year-old son to Angley to be healed of hyperactivity, Angley's yelling at Satan caused the child to cry. In an attempt to calm the boy Angley responded in a caring, fatherly voice, "Honey, Jesus loves you. And I wouldn't hurt you. No. I'm your buddy. I'm your buddy . . . Oh no, don't you cry now."

Shortly, the child ceased crying. The timing of his response and tone of his voice suggested that Angley's concern for the little boy was sincere.

Former President Harry Truman once remarked that "the public is quick to detect and reject the charlatan and the demagogue. It may be deceived for a brief period, but not for long." Concurring with Truman, Eugene White suggests that even a hint of insincerity may result in failure for the speaker (214). If this be true, it is doubtful that Angley's listeners view him as an insincere man, for even today his Akron ministry continues to flourish as it has for the past five decades of existence. Angley is liked by his constituency because he appears to be genuinely concerned for their well-being. The rhetorical features of honesty and sincerity, therefore, go a long way in bolstering his appeal.

ANGLEY'S LOVE AND COMPASSION

Closely related to sincerity is the love that Angley consciously pours out to his followers in his discourse. This, too, helps persuade individuals to join his ministry. For example, Angley frequently discloses in his letters to his partners, "You are loved very, very much by this ministry" (Letter to author, 12 Nov. 1987).

When preaching from the pulpit at Grace Cathedral, Angley is very explicit in telling his television audiences that he loves them. "We love you," he declares. "That's the reason we come to you week after week . . . to be a blessing to you." Jesus' number one mission for all nations is "really close to my heart," says Angley. "We're trying to reach everybody we can." In closing he assures his viewers, "We love you. And God loves you. I pray for you partners day after day" ("The Ernest Angley Hour" 7 Feb. 1988).

Even in the literature that he sends to those who request it, Angley makes a concerted effort to emphasize love. He suggests, for instance, "Through the power of the Cross, your God will move. He loves you; He cares for you. He'll hold you close, breathe upon you and give you strength." Additionally, he urges those who "wake in the mornings feeling unloved, uncared for" to turn to God. "You are precious in [God's] sight," says Angley (*Power of the Cross* 18).

This type of message would appeal to those individuals who have fallen on hard times—the drug addicts, the alcoholics, the poor, and the socially oppressed. Angley is merely filling the void of loneliness and desperation when he tells his viewers how much he cares for them. Thus, love messages help to persuade individuals to become a part of Angley's ministry.

INSPIRATION FOR THE PHYSICALLY MAIMED

For much the same reason that many people find his love appealing, others find hope in Angley's preaching especially those who are physically afflicted. In the Friday night service attended by this writer, Angley consciously exuded hope to the handicapped who were not in short supply. After pointing out that Christ was always busy healing people, he responded, "He is the healing Christ . . . and you know he performs miracles. You know he does. You know that he heals the lame. He is the healing Christ."

Whenever individuals have exhausted their options for recovery, as have some individuals in Angley's healing lines, the only thing left is for them to turn to Angley in hope of receiving a miraculous healing. Angley, for example, responded to one woman who had received no cure after visiting medical authorities, that he believes in good doctors, but that God would take over "when the doctors have done all they can." Simply put, Angley offers hope when all other hope is gone. Or as a friend who accompanied this writer to Angley's Friday night miracles service commented, "Most people there were desperate to solve their problems" (Observation by the author). Thus, when all hope is gone, individuals look to Angley for miraculous, divine healing. Lewis argues that charismatic figures, like Angley, "emerge in times of deprivation and disenfranchisement. Masses of people, feeling they have lost everything, attribute charisma to leaders who give them hope for a better future or a means to regain their losses" ("Charisma and Media Evangelists" 97). This is only one of the many reasons why Angley is a popular figure.

ANGLEY AS THE ULTIMATE LEGITIMIZER

The above description, a concept borrowed from Ernest Bormann, professor of rhetoric at the University of Minnesota, refers to the leader in a drama who embodies, and thereby gives legitimacy to the beliefs and values of the group (401). Overcoming the vicissitudes of life helps to legitimize one's existence. Hence, Angley validates his beliefs and practices to his audience by describing to them the terrible shape his life was in before God wrought miracles on him. As has been noted in previous chapters, this type of testimony as a rhetorical strategy can be a powerful force in persuading others to accept one's position.

Since one of Angley's missions is to win souls to Christ, he himself constantly reminds his listeners of his own positive conversion experience in hope that they, too, might be compelled to accept Christ. "When I was eighteen, the Lord saved me," he relates (de Groot G-4). "I shall remember forever that night in my teens when I took Jesus home with me. Never have I let Him go. It was the greatest night of my life! I wanted to tell the whole world I met the Master! I'm cleansed, saved, born again! I've been to Calvary!" (Angley, *The Power of the Cross* 8). Angley recounts how, upon leaving the altar the night of his conversion, he left on a different road (i.e., "the love road" of Christ) than the one on which he came (Observation by the author). "I knew that night I'd never be the same. I had found the king of my life and for my life" ("The Ernest Angley Hour" 23 Aug. 1987).

Perhaps Angley's conversion would never have occurred if he had not had others around him to set the example. "Through my Dad's life, my mom's life, my two oldest sisters, I saw the star shining bright to show me the way. As a little boy I'd go in and sit there and listen to good Sunday school teachers filled with the Spirit of God. And you know a lot of saints of God kept that star shining bright for me to see." He further suggests how the Lord chose him. "He wanted me, that little ol' boy called Ernest Angley. . . . He wanted me so he could direct my paths and make them plain paths that would lead to heaven" ("The Ernest Angley Hour" 23 Aug. 1987). This kind of testimony demonstrates that not only does Angley believe that his message about salvation is valid but that God himself personally called him to the ministry. In other words, God has put his stamp of approval on Angley. The logic runs something like this: "If what Angley says is true (and to his listeners there is no reason to believe otherwise), then God must have personally chosen Angley for his ministry." Lewis contends that followers who are "driven by the frustrations and stress of their situational crises" are often drawn to a leader like Angley who claims to have received a "special calling" from God (103).

In addition to the testimonies surrounding his conversion, Angley consciously attempts to legitimize his teachings on miracles through personal examples. For instance, besides relaying the fact that God cured him of an ulcerated stomach, Angley reveals how God also healed him of a bone disease. "I would have probably just had one leg today, just one. The other one would have been artificial had it not been for the Lord," he contends. Angley describes the "disease that almost destroyed me as a child" as an awful pain, something that he could "never put in words." Pointing out that the pain was so excruciating that he has never really "been able to describe it," Angley narrates how it felt like "some wild animal of some kind gnawing on the bone of my leg, that the flesh was gone and it was just gnawing, gnawing on the bone" ("The Ernest Angley Hour" 23 Aug. 1987).

His affliction lasted for a long period of time. "My mother would sleep with me and she would pray into the wee hours of the morning," he remembers. Then after many nights of prayer, "King Jesus came and made me whole, made me well. I knew he could heal. I didn't doubt his healing power. I knew it. I had a good leg," he relates ("The Ernest Angley Hour" 23 Aug. 1987).

Like those of other faith healers in the twentieth century, Angley's tales of personal healings serve to persuade his audience to believe that miracles are true and should, therefore, be accepted. Hence, one does not have to wonder why it is that Angley has such a large turnout for his Friday night miracle services. People from all across the country and Canada come expecting to receive their miracle, just as Angley has received his. In effect Angley is the ultimate legitimizer of miracles as well as of salvation. Lewis concurs with the above conclusion when he suggests that "fanatical followers seem to be drawn to those leaders whose defects have been surmounted and those who exist despite possible difficulties." Faith healers use these types of testimonies, contends Lewis, "to gain [a] charismatic bond with their audiences" (103). Certainly, this strategy—which appears to be conscious—works for Angley.

In addition to personal testimonies surrounding his salvation and miracles, another type of attestation that legitimizes Angley as a man of God is his rise from poverty. Angley recounts how "God prepared me for the hard places." "I grew up fast in a big family, in a poor home where I had to dig, work and fight for everything I got. I learned not to accept defeat, not to be overcome by discouragement" (*Untying God's Hands* 65). In his interview with Fred Griffith, Angley states, "I wasn't born in wealth, but we had a lot of love, and I never associated money and happiness together. We had a lot of happiness, a lot of love, but very little money." He relates how, as a boy, he had "but one hand-me-down sweater to wear as I walked, shaking and chilled to the bone, over a mile to school in the winter. I had forgotten about that sweater," says Angley, "until the Lord took me back to my boyhood, showing how He had gotten me ready for His work." According to Angley, the Lord "was getting me ready for a ministry on which I would never turn back, never say no to God or find a task too hard." He suggests how being "accustomed to battles [and] hardships and being in want . . . toughened me" (*Untying God's Hands* 65).

Much like many other faith healers, such as William Branham, Oral Roberts, and A. A. Allen, Ernest Angley's life is a rags-to-riches story. For decades Grace Cathedral, with its elaborate decorations, served to remind one of his success. Now his new Grace Cathedral serves a similar function. Because God was preparing him for the ministry through poverty, and since Angley is no longer poor, his followers naturally would think that God has anointed Angley for the ministry. In other words God has blessed Angley with wealth to confirm him as a servant. Thus, when one visits Angley's new Grace Cathedral with its plush interior or when one sees a well-groomed, finely-clad man stroll onto the stage, it becomes difficult for Angley's constituency to believe that God has not called him to preach and minister to the physically afflicted. They, therefore, acquiesce to his message.

ANGLEY'S APPEARANCE AND PERFORMANCE

One of the first things that one notices about Ernest Angley is his appearance. Because of his looks, he has been the subject of frequent parodies ("A Beginner's Guide to Television Evangelists" 157–61). Laura Haferd of *The [Akron] Beacon Journal* suggests, "You can't call him 'the inimitable Ernest Angley' because everywhere you look some comedian or car dealer is doing an imitation of him" ("Pitching and Preaching" B-1).

Angley is a portly man about five feet, eight inches tall. Haferd suggests that with his stooped shoulders he reminds one of Richard Nixon. Occasionally, she suggests, he looks like a "peeved Richard Simmons" ("Pitching and Preaching B-1). Commenting on his stage presence, Randi confesses, "To me he is a ludicrous figure, but to his parishioners he is a God-inspired preacher" (238).

Angley frequently dresses conservatively, although in the spring and summer he regularly wears white and light-colored suits. His appearance is always neat, however. The Friday night this writer visited Grace Cathedral, Angley was wearing a charcoal-colored suit with a light blue shirt and a pink silk tie accompanied by a matching silk handkerchief protruding from his upper coat pocket. Square cufflinks, an indistinguishable watchband, and a gold wedding ring that he still wears periodically reflected the bright ceiling lights, as did his immaculately polished black shoes. Except for the shirt collar that flared outward at the ends, Angley's attire could easily have been mistaken for something out of a gentleman's fashion magazine.

Angley's dress is always overshadowed by his style of preaching, however. Speaking with a tense, nasal twang, he frequently darts to the right or to the left of the podium with his body. His hands are continually in motion. The sudden upward jerks of his head reveal a gleam in his eyes reflected from the auditorium lights as he constantly furrows his eyebrows and wrinkles his forehead, changing his facial expressions.

Neuendorf and Ableman suggest that, second only to James Robison, Ernest Angley had the greatest amount of facial intensity of all preachers in their study of fourteen popular televangelists (51–52). Speaking, by and large, in a conversational tone, Angley occasionally yells at the top of his voice to emphasize the seriousness of a point. Neuendorf and Ableman point out that Angley's primary communication type is conversational. In other words, "Angley is more likely to assume a conversational tone" rather than speak bombastically. Despite this, he was still rated fourth in vocal intensity and third in overall intensity among the fourteen ministers Neuendorf and Ableman studied (47, 56).

In a word, Ernest Angley is interesting to watch. His professional appearance coupled with his conversational, yet at times, serious tone probably contributes to his overall appeal. Despite any negative points that one might make about his style and delivery, these probably in no way impede his message to his parishioners. In his book *Criticism of Oral Rhetoric*, Carroll Arnold points out that generally, "visible action does not harm [a speaker's] communication" and that "certain deficiencies in the audible code, though listeners consider them unpleasant, do not affect comprehension." The conclusion that one should draw from this, suggests Arnold, is not that speakers should not strive for excellence in delivery but that "in the whole complex of content, style, arrangement, and delivery no one presentational element . . . is likely to affect the outcome significantly." He goes on to suggest that "the nonverbal aspects of speaking will probably affect listeners' responses very little unless verbal and nonverbal behaviors seem inconsistent or mutually reinforcing to an unusual degree" (217–18).

It is difficult to judge in every case what effect Angley's style and delivery have on those observing him. To some, like James Randi, Angley is indeed "a ludicrous figure" (238). For others, though, especially for his regular viewers and parishioners, Angley's style and delivery merely serve to reinforce his message. Because of his style and delivery, Ernest Angley probably continues to appeal to audiences who either flock to Grace Cathedral for the weekend or tune in to his weekly and daily television programs. Lewis notes that "While the accents and strange linguistic behavior of . . . Ernest Angley . . . may be the basis for derisive commentary and caricature by critics, this 'strange' aura may be an attraction for the fanatical follower" ("Charisma and Media Evangelists" 103).

CONCLUSION

Ernest Angley is persuasive to his followers for a number of reasons, all of which work interdependently. Besides the fact that he is interesting to watch due to his smooth style and delivery, he appears to be a humble and sincere man who offers love and hope to the downtrodden. Angley's recounting of his own experiences in overcoming life's hardships also contributes to his appeal. These experiences legitimize his teachings and validate his existence as preacher and faith healer.

Although his behavior to many outsiders may appear idiosyncratic at best and downright strange at worst, Angley's followers do not perceive him as such. Instead, they view him as a convicted man of God's calling, and, because he is, flock to his weekend services and/or tune in to his weekly telecast. Despite the fact that his popularity is not as great as other contemporary televangelists, Angley is, nonetheless, a national and international figure who has captured the hearts of thousands of people, both in the United States and abroad, most of whom probably look to him to help them repair their broken or unhappy life. Any serious discussion of faith healers, or even televangelists for that matter, would be incomplete if it did not include

Akron's elderly minister and long-time Pentecostal resident, Ernest Angley.

REFERENCES

" 'Angel' of Grace Cathedral Dies." *[Akron] Beacon Journal* 29 Dec. 1970: n.p.

Angley, Ernest. "Abide in God's Love." *The Power of the Holy Ghost* Aug. 1987: 2–12.

———. *Cell 15: The Imprisonment of Ernest Angley*. Akron, OH: Winston Press, 1984.

———. *Confidence*. Akron, OH: Winston Press, 1988.

———. *The Ernest Angley Hour* (Television Program). WHMB. Indianapolis. 23 Aug. 1987.

———. *The Ernest Angley Hour* (Television Program). WHMB. Indianapolis. 7 Feb. 1988.

———. *The Ernest Angley Hour* (Television Program). WHMB. Indianapolis. 21 Feb. 1988.

———. *Faith in God Heals the Sick*. Akron, OH: Winston Press, 1983.

———. *The Greatness of the Fire of the Holy Spirit*. Akron, OH: Winston Press, 1987.

———. Interview with Fred Griffith. "The Morning Exchange." WEWS-TV. Cleveland, OH. Mar. 1988.

———. Letter to Author. 12 Nov. 1987.

———. Letter to Author. Feb. 1988.

———. *Lukewarm Christians*. Akron, OH: Winston Press, 1987.

———. *The Ninety and Nine Club* (Television Broadcast). WBNX. Cable Channel 8. Akron, OH. 23 Sept. 1997.

———. *The Power of the Cross*. Akron, OH: Winston Press, 1987.

———. *Untying God's Hands*. Akron, OH: Winston Press, 1977.

Arbitron Ratings Co. Chicago. May 1987.

Arnold, Carroll C. *Criticism of Oral Rhetoric*. Columbus, OH: Charles E. Merrill, 1974.

"A Beginners Guide to Television Evangelists." *Playboy* October 1980: 157–61.

Bormann, Ernest G. "Fantasy and Rhetorical Vision: The Rhetorical Criticism of Social Reality." *Quarterly Journal of Speech* 58 (1972): 396–407.

de Groot, John. "In Rev. Angley's Gloryland: Miracles 4 Times a Week." *[Akron] Beacon Journal* 5 June 1966: G-4.

Haferd, Laura. "The 'Faith-healing' Arrest That Did Wonders." *[Akron] Beacon Journal* 3 April 1987: B4.

————. "Pitching and Preaching." *[Akron] Beacon Journal* 3 April 1987: B1, B4.

Lewis, Todd V. "Charisma and Media Evangelists: An Explication and Model of Communication Influence." *The Southern Communication Journal* 54 (Fall, 1988): 93–111.

Neuendorf, Kimberly, and Robert Ableman. "Televangelism: A Look at Communicator Style." *Journal of Religious Studies* 13 (1985): 41–59.

Randi, James. *The Faith Healers*. Buffalo, NY: Prometheus Books, 1987.

White, Eugene E. *Basic Public Speaking*. New York: Macmillan Publishing Co., 1984.

CHAPTER SIX

The Red-Haired "Preacher Lady" from Concordia, Missouri: Kathryn Kuhlman

There she often stood, backstage, alone with her thoughts, pacing back and forth, butterflies swarming in her stomach, praying with all of her might that God would be with her. To hear her tell it, the strain was almost unbearable. Just minutes before whisking onto the stage in her long, flowing gowns with billowy sleeves to greet thousands who had come, in part, to gaze upon this tall, red-haired evangelist, Kathryn Kuhlman would "die a thousand deaths," petrified that, in her words, the Holy Spirit, might not have arrived to carry her through the upcoming miracle service. How could she face people who had come hundreds—in some cases thousands—of miles to be healed if the Holy Spirit were not there to help her? Prior to each service she felt utterly helpless and completely dependent upon "the power of the Holy Spirit" ("In Tribute to Kathryn Kuhlman"). She occasionally remarked that she walked onto the stage as fast as she could because she could not wait to get under the Spirit's influence to rid herself of her pre-performance anxieties ("An Hour with Kathryn Kuhlman").

For over five decades Kathryn Kuhlman, world-renowned evangelist and faith healer, a term she abhorred ("Healing in the Spirit"), packed large auditoriums and sanctuaries wherever she went often

Kathryn Kuhlman preaching in Mabee Center on the campus of Oral Roberts University, September 30, 1973. Courtesy of The Kathryn Kuhlman Foundation and Billy Graham Center Archives, Wheaton College, Wheaton, Illinois. Photographer: Doug Grandstaff. Reprinted with permission of The Kathryn Kuhlman Foundation and Mrs. Earlene Grandstaff.

filling up hours before the services began. None of her contemporaries, with the exception of Oral Roberts, was as well-known to the general public or as well respected in the Pentecostal and Charismatic world as was Kathryn Kuhlman.

Early in her career some called her "America's greatest young lady preacher" (Buckingham 78). Those closest to her often called her "a handmaiden of God" ("An Hour with Kathryn Kuhlman"). *Time* once referred to her as a "veritable one-woman shrine of Lourdes" ("Miracle Woman" 62). *Christianity Today* observed that "Not since Aimee Semple McPherson has a woman religious figure been recognized and appreciated so far and wide" ("Healing in the Spirit" 4). So rhetorically compelling was she to audiences that *People* once suggested, "She has so mastered the art of selling that even if one is a skeptic, one cannot look and listen without being fascinated by this woman . . . (Farr 13). Indeed, Kathryn Kuhlman had one of the most prominent healing ministries of the entire twentieth century. There can be no doubt, therefore, that she belongs in any discussion of twentieth-century healing evangelists.

KUHLMAN'S BACKGROUND

Kathryn Kuhlman's story is, in some respects, similar to Aimee Semple McPherson's. Born the third of four children on a farm outside the small town of Concordia, Missouri on May 9, 1907, to Joseph and Emma Walkenhorst Kuhlman, Kathryn Johanna Kuhlman was raised by her mother in the Methodist church. She often relayed how one Sunday morning when she "wasn't quite fourteen," she was born again in the "little Methodist church" in Concordia ("An Hour With Kathryn Kuhlman"; Lairdon 33–34). Her father, who once served as Mayor of Concordia, was a non-practicing Baptist who had little use for religion and even less use for preachers. According to her, he "despised" and "hated them" ("An Hour with Kathryn Kuhlman").

In 1924, around the age of sixteen or seventeen, she dropped out of high school at the end of her tenth-grade year and left home to preach in the Pacific Northwest with her older sister Myrtle and brother-in-law Everett Parrott, an evangelist in his own right. It was not until 1928 that Kathryn decided to break away from her sister and brother-in-law and begin her own ministry when a local preacher in Boise, Idaho gave her and her pianist Helen Gulliford a chance to hold services in a mission that had been converted from a pool hall.

Billed as "God's Girls," for the next five years they held revivals in small, crossroads towns across Idaho.

On August 27, 1933 Kathryn and Helen settled down, if at least, only temporarily. They began a ministry in Denver in a vacant warehouse owned by Montgomery Ward, not far from the state capital. The congregation grew. On May 30, 1935, Kuhlman held the dedication service of her Denver Revival Tabernacle, a renovated horse barn and warehouse on West Ninth and Acoma Street, replete with a neon sign over the top of it, announcing "PRAYER CHANGES THINGS." In time, the Tabernacle would develop prison and retirement-home ministries as well as bus services to the assemblies. For the next five years, thousands of people flocked to the Tabernacle (Warner 47–70; Buckingham 7–71). By all outward indications, Kathryn Kuhlman's Denver ministry appeared to be thriving. But its success was to be short-lived.

Controversy soon surrounded Kuhlman when in Mason City, Iowa on Oct. 18, 1938—against the advice of those closest to her—she married Burroughs A. Waltrip, a dark-haired, handsome Texas evangelist who had initially come to Denver to hold a revival. Waltrip wound up staying for thirty weeks during 1935 and 1936.

The problem lay in the fact that Waltrip, eight years Kathryn's senior, was married with two young sons. Eventually Waltrip left Denver to begin a church in Mason City, Iowa. Kathryn followed shortly thereafter to help with the preaching and assist in raising money for his newly built "Radio Chapel." While together in Iowa, Waltrip told Kuhlman that his wife had deserted him leaving them free to marry which they did over the strong protests of Kathryn's advisors. After her marriage to "Mister," as Kathryn affectionately referred to Waltrip, Kuhlman left the work in Denver (which, by now, was splitting up when the congregants heard of Kathryn's marriage) to join her new husband as co-pastor in Mason City. But in Mason City their reception as husband and wife was really no better. A little over six months after their marriage, Waltrip preached his last sermon at "Radio Chapel" on Sunday evening, May 14, 1939. That evening also marked the Waltrips' ignominious departure from town (see Warner 81–99; Buckingham 75–86).

In her heart of hearts, Kathryn believed her marriage to Waltrip was wrong. The guilt was too much for her to bear. While living in Los Angeles in 1944 and feeling what she described as the weight of God's call upon her, Kuhlman walked out on Waltrip. While taking a walk at approximately four o'clock on a Saturday afternoon in 1944, Kuhlman claims that she had "come to a dead end" in her life. No longer could she deny what she felt was God's call for her to return to the ministry. Three days later she bought a one-way ticket to Franklin, Pennsylvania where she had been invited to hold a two-week revival. Like a scene out of some Hollywood movie, she left Waltrip standing on the platform at the train station. Her divorce with Waltrip would eventually become final in 1948. With the exception of a valentine she received in 1970, she would never hear from him again. Between 1944 and 1946 Kuhlman held revivals across the South and Midwest before returning to Franklin, Pennsylvania to settle down for a few years (Buckingham 85–106; Lairdon 59).

Despite the fact that the first miracle ostensibly occurred in one of her services in Franklin on April 27, 1947, while she preached on the power of the Holy Spirit, it was not until July 4, 1948, that Kuhlman held her first "miracle service" in Carnegie Hall on the Northwest side of Pittsburgh. This was to be the first of many held there during the next three decades. In 1950 Kuhlman moved permanently from Sugar Creek, near Franklin, to Pittsburgh, which was to be the base of her operations for the next twenty-five years. In the early 1950s she held meetings in Akron and Youngstown, Ohio. Aside from holding services in Carnegie Hall in Pittsburgh from 1948 through 1967, she also used the First Presbyterian Church which was offered to her by Dr. Robert Lamont, the church's pastor, after Carnegie Hall became unavailable for her use. In 1965 she began holding monthly healing services at the Shrine Auditorium in Los Angeles, the location where she preached her last sermon in November 1975, shortly before her death a few months later (Buckingham 107–35; Warner 113–69).

Prior to her death, she was heard on more than fifty radio stations and seen on more than sixty television stations ("Kathryn Kuhlman . . . Dies in Tulsa"). All told, she produced over 4,000 radio programs and 500 television shows during her lifetime (Warner 193).

On December 28, 1975, in Tulsa, Oklahoma Kuhlman underwent open heart surgery to replace her mitral valve. After a prolonged stay in the Hillcrest Medical Center she died on February 20, 1976, of "pulmonary hypertension." Like McPherson, she was buried in Forest Lawn Memorial Park in Glendale, California ("Kathryn Kuhlman: To God Be the Glory" 7). Well-known evangelist Oral Roberts, who spoke at Kuhlman's funeral, praised her as "the greatest evangelist of the ministry of God's miracle power in my lifetime" ("The Late

Kathryn Kuhlman"). With her passing, the Pentecostal and charismatic world had lost one of their most notable public figures of the twentieth century.

Much of Kuhlman's success as a twentieth-century faith healer lies in the fact that she followed a rhetorical pattern—whether consciously or unconsciously—like those who preceded her. This is not to say that Kuhlman did not have her own style, nor is it to imply that she ran her services the same way that others did. In general, though, the types of proofs that she offered to her followers—those critical elements that make a rhetor popular and subsequently induce belief—were similar to those who came before her, as well as those of her contemporaries. And, for the most part, many of the same kinds of people who flocked to Kathryn's services were like those in attendance at meetings of previous healing evangelists.

KUHLMAN'S AUDIENCE

Judging by the types of people who appear in the handful of videos made of Kathryn Kuhlman's healing services, one can deduce that they came from all economic classes—some well-off financially, some poor, perhaps mostly just middle class, though. And while not foolproof evidence in every case, nonverbal artifacts such as clothing and automobiles bespeak of their wealth, or in many cases, the lack thereof. After attending a Kathryn Kuhlman crusade himself, Oral Roberts once remarked, "I looked around. It was a different audience then [sic] came to my meetings. You could tell this was an audience that had touched the so-called top people as well as the more common like myself" (Buckingham 252).

Additionally, those who followed Kuhlman came from various ethnic and religious backgrounds—blacks, whites, Latinos, Asians; believers and unbelievers; Protestants, Jews, and Catholics. In fact, Warner points out that by drawing so many Catholics to her services, Kuhlman helped "bridge gaps" between Protestants and Catholics (163). He suggests that Kuhlman realized that people "from all walks of life" flocked to her services, "from the poor to the super-rich, from the unknown to the world renowned, from the ungodly to the deeply spiritual" (212).

Perhaps more significant than these, however, were those physically afflicted who, not surprisingly, came in search of a miracle. One would obviously expect these types at any healing revival. In his popular book *Healing: A Doctor in Search of a Miracle*, medical doctor William Nolen recounts how many people who attended a Kathryn Kuhlman crusade while he served as an usher had turned to her out of desperation. "I've seen some sad sights in my life, but few that could match the one that greeted me when the [elevator] doors opened and our first charges arrived." Nolen tells of how he saw stroke victims "drooling from the corners of their mouth," children "crippled by birth defects," and paralyzed cancer patients with "withered arms or legs," among others. "Every patient I saw," reveals Nolen, "except of course those who were retarded, had the desperate look of those who have all but given up—who are nearly . . . resigned to their fate." Nolen suggests that people of all social classes eventually "go looking for salvation elsewhere when a medical doctor admits he can't help" (7, 53–55). One of her biographers, Jamie Buckingham, once observed about Kuhlman, "On a planet ravaged by disease and spiritual darkness she represented that one ingredient without which mankind is doomed—hope" (1). Likewise, *Christianity Today* remarked how Kuhlman "increasingly represented the last great hope of the desperately ill," of those "given up by medical science" ("Healing in the Spirit" 4).

Warner reveals that in time, "the number of deathly sick people" who came to Kuhlman's crusades "multiplied many times over." "The Shrine Auditorium became a literal outpatient clinic, except this clinic was filled with terminal patients in wheelchairs and hospital beds. Many of them were there against their doctor's orders." Warner also points out that most would exit in the same condition in which they entered (211).

Although she was well aware that most afflicted people who came into her services were not healed, she continued nonetheless to believe it was God's will for her to help miraculously cure the infirmities of those who sought Him ("Baptism of the Holy Spirit"; "I Believe in Miracles"; "Why Aren't Some Healed? no. 2").

KUHLMAN'S HUMILITY AND CREDIT TO GOD

Like the other figures in this book, one thing that made Kuhlman popular with her audiences while simultaneously serving to persuade them was her willingness to give God the credit for any healings. Pages could be filled with quotations of Kuhlman articulating to her followers that it was God and not her who healed. Kuhlman went to great lengths to make this known to her followers. In her book *I Believe in Miracles*, for example, Kuhlman made it clear: "If you believe that I, as an individual, have any powers to heal, you are dead wrong. . . . I can lead you to the great physician—the rest is left with you and God" (1). On another occasion she remarked, "Kathryn Kuhlman herself knew better than anyone else in the whole world that she had no healing virtue, that she had no healing powers. . . . I had no power to heal if my life depended upon it" ("In Tribute to Kathryn Kuhlman"). For Kathryn the power was in the Holy Spirit. When she began her services she often prayed, "And we vow . . . to be so careful to give you all the praise and all the honor and all the glory for everything that the Holy Spirit does in this place of worship today." While praying, she reminded her audience that God will not share the "glory" or the "praise." Therefore, Kuhlman prayed, "We vow to give you the glory . . ." (*Dry Land, Living Waters*).

In addition to giving God the credit for any healings that she believed occurred Kuhlman continued her humble stance before her audiences by reminding them that she was one of the most ordinary people alive, just a girl from the small town of Concordia, Missouri. Like Aimee Semple McPherson who claimed to be merely a girl from the farm, so Kuhlman, too, was able to identify with the common people by using a similar theme. Kathryn repeatedly asserted, "There's not a woman living today who's more ordinary than the one who's standing before you now. I know from whence I've come . . . a little crossroads of a town in Concordia, Missouri." She disclosed to audiences that in her mind she is "the most unlikely person in the whole world that God would use" ("Baptism of the Holy Spirit"). In one of her last sermons preached shortly before her death Kuhlman lamented, "I know better than anyone else from where I come—from a little crossroads town in Missouri with a population of twelve hundred people. I had nothing. I was born without talent." She told of how she reasoned with God, "If you can take nothing and use it, then here's nothing. Take it" ("God's Generals," vol. 7, part II). Once, after confessing that she was born "without talent," she proceeded to disclose that she "always had an inferiority complex about my looks, born with this fuzz on my head." Because she did not see herself as intrinsically talented or good looking, she stated that she would not "walk across the street" to see herself (*Dry Land, Living Waters*).

Kuhlman was not ashamed of where she was from. Rather, she seemed to be proud of her background. She frequently and quite fondly alluded to her upbringing, telling stories about her mother and father and her escapades in small-town middle America. She told, for example, about those "long Sunday afternoons" in Concordia when she and her girlfriend Maxine would walk the railroad tracks to Emma, Missouri three miles away. She reminded them that today, however, she is "walking the rail" with God, being careful not to lose her balance (*I Believe in Miracles* vol. III). Audiences delighted in the spiritual applications that she drew from her homey stories about her humble beginnings.

She often told of having spent the night in a turkey house or not having much to eat early in her work while still a struggling young evangelist. Indeed early on times were hard for Kuhlman and later in her ministry she freely shared those memories. It was as if she understood the rhetorical value of such stories, of how her audiences could identify with her, of how they would see her not as some untouchable persona but as a humble servant of God who had grown up in a small town and who, for the most part, had experienced a normal childhood before launching out into an uncaring world before being tried by fire, like what perhaps many of her followers had experienced in pre-World War II America. Buckingham contends that Kathryn's "constantly telling all those stories about sleeping in turkey houses . . . and using the public baths for a nickel when she was too poor to afford a room with a shower . . . gave her . . . the needed identification with the poor, while allowing her the luxury of living like a queen" (247). So, whether it was Kuhlman disavowing personal powers, giving credit to God, or relaying the ordinariness of her person, her humility served her well in attracting and maintaining a following.

Kuhlman's humility, like that of the other healing revivalists in this book, appeared to be sincere. She was not a fake. She did not feign humility simply because she believed it was good business, just because she believed it would somehow boost her ministry. Rather, her humility appeared to be genuine. It was because of her sincerity that others accepted her. Jimmy McDonald, Kathryn's long-time soloist, once remarked, "When Kathryn Kuhlman said that she was the most surprised person in the world as to what happened during a healing and that she had absolutely nothing to do with it, she was not just being humble. She really meant it. She always gave the glory to the Holy Spirit" (*The Kathryn Kuhlman I Knew* 115).

ECUMENICALISM, HUMOR, AND GOOD WILL

As has been suggested already Kuhlman preached to Protestants, Catholics, and Jews alike. She made it clear that all were welcome at her assemblies. Moreover, she often did it with a humorous twist. No doubt, in this way, she elevated her popularity.

In her usual self-deprecating way Kathryn commented that "this is the most unorthodox ministry in the whole world," which evoked a teasing "Amen" from Jimmy McDonald. "What do you mean by 'Amen?' You don't have to agree so heartily," Kathryn jokingly chastised. Her audience roared with laughter as Kuhlman, like a stand-up comedian with a grin on her face, basked in the glow of her audience's acceptance. She understood how much her followers loved her humor. Kuhlman was humorous because she believed that the Holy Spirit had a sense of humor. "I know that He does," she confessed ("Baptism of the Holy Spirit").

In explaining her unorthodox ministry Kuhlman noted, "You see, we don't care whether you're Protestant, Catholic, Jew or Gentile. It doesn't make any difference to God, so why should it make any difference to us?" To this the audience erupted in applause. Kuhlman went on to thank a Catholic priest for holding a Mass for her recently. She then humorously followed by saying she would not be surprised if she were invited to a synagogue before leaving town. And she promised to go if invited, much to the delight of those in attendance who laughed and applauded (*Dry Land, Living Waters*).

Once Kuhlman seriously commented to a Jewish man whose wife came to the platform claiming healing of multiple sclerosis, "If you only knew of the love that I have for the Jewish people because I know the covenants and the promises that Jehovah God made to the seed of Israel. O bless them. Dear wonderful Jesus, just bless them. Just bless them" ("In Tribute to Kathryn Kuhlman"). In fact it was common for someone of the Jewish faith to walk onto the podium crying and claiming that he or she had been healed, proof that Kathryn's ecumenicalism was working (*Dry Land, Living Waters*).

When listening to the preaching of Kathryn Kuhlman it does not take one long to understand how much she cared for people of all faiths. She embraced practically everyone, regardless of their creed. Once, for example, she reasoned with an audience, "you may not see eye to eye with me" on a number of different issues, such as divine healing and the rapture of the church, but if a person has had a born again experience, "you're my brother" ("Baptism of the Holy Spirit"). On another occasion, she ecumenically, albeit jokingly, suggested that her "Grandpa Walkenhorst" was going to get "the shock of his life" when and if he gets to heaven to know that "some Baptists are there" ("An Hour with Kathryn Kuhlman"). This remark brought a round of laughter from her audience.

Warner points out that Kuhlman did not condemn people. She did not preach against such vices as drinking and smoking for fear that she might alienate someone (161). Instead, she chose to be positive, believing that a positive message that Jesus heals both spiritually and physically would create more good will. If good will toward her audiences, as shown through her excellent sense of humor, positive confirmation of different religions, and avoidance of condemnation raises a speaker's credibility, certainly Kuhlman's ethos on these accounts was high. How could one not like a speaker with a sense of humor who was willing to embrace religious differences as well as similarities? Kuhlman seemed to understand these rhetorical dynamics well and often played her humor and ecumenical cards to gain and sustain a following. Anything else might result in ill will and this was the last thing Kuhlman wanted.

TESTIMONIES, EXAMPLES, AND PHYSICAL DEMONSTRATIONS AS RHETORICAL PROOF

As has been suggested in each of the previous chapters, one of the most effective rhetorical techniques for convincing listeners to believe in healings is the testimony of someone who has experienced the healing. And what is more, if an audience can see the individual who claims some sort of healing, walking up and down, bending over and touching their toes, or running about the stage like a colt frolicking in a field, then they have even more reason to believe. Kuhlman understood the value of these techniques and used them to induce belief.

Unlike Roberts, Allen, and other healers in the first half of the twentieth century who had individuals walk across the stage to have hands laid on them before they could be healed, Kuhlman simply relied on the Holy Spirit to heal people while still in their seats as she stood on the platform and preached. Once the sermon was over ushers, trained to be on the lookout, would then corral these individuals into lines at the sides of the stage where, in time, Kathryn would call them forward and query them in front of the entire audience about their healing. She would then lay her hands upon them to slay them in the spirit, at which point they would fall backward into the arms of a waiting usher who would gently lower them to the ground.

Once, after supposedly healing a foot ailment, Kuhlman asked the individual who stomped her foot on the ground as empirical proof, "Is it completely loosened?" to which the person responded in the affirmative. "And there's no pain?" she continued. "And you weren't expecting it at all?" "How long have you had this condition?" All of these questions were obviously asked in an attempt to prove to the audience that what they were witnessing was indeed a miracle. She did this, she reasoned, because she had seen so many healings in so many services that she took "so much for granted" and forgot what it was like to be in the audience. Kuhlman once confessed, "You have to see with your own eyes to believe" (*Dry Land, Living Waters*).

In addition to having people physically demonstrate their healing on stage often Kuhlman would ask if there were someone in the audience who knew the person being healed so that he or she could vouch for the individual's healing. Kuhlman claimed that she wanted the person to "verify it [the healing]" "because I don't want anybody to believe that it isn't just that way. . . . You understand why I do it." In one instance Kuhlman interviewed a man whose wife claimed to receive a healing, a man who admitted to being "very skeptical" of miracles prior to the start of the service. After seeing his wife on stage walking around without her brace the man testified to Kuhlman, "I can't help but believe" ("In Tribute to Kathryn Kuhlman").

Not only did Kuhlman rely on personal testimonies to convince her followers of healing, but she also cited example after example of miracles that she herself supposedly witnessed. It was common, for instance, for Kathryn to report to her audience on a woman whose tumor "literally dissolved in her body" while she was sitting during one of Kuhlman's sermons. "Since that time," suggested Kuhlman, "literally thousands and thousands and thousands have [been] healed just sitting here in the auditorium. Explain it? All I can tell you is the presence of the Holy Spirit is there to heal" ("In Tribute to Kathryn Kuhlman"). By telling these stories Kuhlman raised the ex- pectation level of those in attendance, making them susceptible to believe in the miraculous. Warner contends that Kuhlman "saw re- deeming value in spilling the less than noble details of a new convert's past or the grave physical problems of people who had been healed—

no doubt to convince the seeker and skeptic alike that with God all things are possible" (107).

Not only did she orally cite case after case of healings, but she frequently reported them in print, although unlike other healers she did not publish a monthly magazine. Kathryn's popular book *I Believe in Miracles*, for example, is little more than chapter after chapter of cases of people who claimed to have been healed of one ailment or another. Her book *God Can Do It Again* also recounts example after example of people who report to have been healed while attending one of Kuhlman's services. *Twilight and Dawn* and *Never Too Late* are other stories of individuals who believe they were healed as a result of their association with Kuhlman.

Like all other faith healers of the twentieth century, there can be little doubt that Kathryn understood the power of personal testimony in selling healing to others for she packed not only her stages but her books as well with examples of people who claim to have received a miraculous cure. If there were one thing above all others that Kuhlman understood about persuading an audience, it was the value of personal testimony and demonstration. She relied on these proofs greatly throughout her career.

KUHLMAN'S USE OF DOCTORS

In addition to physical demonstrations and personal testimonies Kuhlman occasionally pointed out that there were doctors in her audiences who could verify healings. In other words, if a listener did not believe an individual's testimony or what was being demonstrated physically on stage, certainly audiences' respect for the medical profession would induce them to believe.

In her Las Vegas crusade of May 3, 1975, one of only four tapes available of Kuhlman's healing services, she explicitly made known to her followers that doctors were in the house. Reminding her audience that the doctors were "distinguished men" "on the front row" (one from the prestigious Johns Hopkins Hospital in Baltimore no less), Kuhlman told the doctors, and by extension the audience, how glad she was that they were sitting where they "won't miss anything." She wanted her followers to know that she had nothing to hide, that she was not afraid of the fact that doctors were available to disaffirm on the spot that miracles had occurred if such were to be the case. "I see a couple of you who first came to the services as skeptics," con-

tinued Kuhlman. Then calling them by name to insure the audience
that she knew them, Kuhlman suggested, "Dr. Casdorph, you were
one of the greatest [skeptics] that I have ever had. There were times
I could have killed you." The audience erupted in laughter. Then,
turning to a female doctor, Kuhlman said, "Dr. Frymann, you came
as a great skeptic, and you had not been trained to believe these
miracles."

Later in the service Kuhlman would call these individuals to the
stage to verify whether miraculous healings had occurred. After Dr.
Frymann examined a woman who claimed to be healed of facial paralysis, Kuhlman asked, "What do you find, doctor?" "I don't find
any evidence of any paralysis," responded Dr. Frymann. "Give her a
great big applause," commanded Kathryn, at which point the audience began clapping (*Dry Land, Living Waters*).

Later, a scientist came on stage claiming that he miraculously had
his hearing restored. The man told Kuhlman that he wanted her to
forget the fact that he was a scientist. Kuhlman turned to the audience
and asked them if they heard what he had just told her. Then she
reminded them, "The two hardest people in the world to convince
[are] a doctor and a scientist" (*Dry Land, Living Waters*). Kuhlman
was demonstrating that the healings in her services had been verified
by two of the most credible professions in the world—that of a scientist and a medical doctor. She realized that to do so would go a
long way in proving to the most hardened skeptic that what she was
doing was indeed genuine and legitimate. Kuhlman understood the
value of these professions in vouching for miracles and employed
them as rhetorical pawns in her crusades whenever she could. No
doubt, for the vast majority of those in attendance, this strategy
worked. After all, for many people, especially those with little or no
education, if a doctor or scientist says it is so, it must be.

Evidence that personal testimonies and the presence of doctors in
Kuhlman's meetings convinced those in her audiences to believe can
be found in Gwen Lanning's book *Twilight and Dawn*. Lanning, a
Baptist, claims she was healed of bone cancer after visiting a Kathryn
Kuhlman crusade and hearing the testimony of a woman who claimed
to have been healed of "a rare blood disease." Lanning records, "I
had wanted to believe but found it difficult until I heard Judy's testimony. Then, as she was about finished, she turned and said, "If you
don't believe what I am saying, ask my doctor. He is here and will
verify all I have said." Lanning continues, "She pointed out into the

auditorium and a distinguished looking man rose to his feet, nodding his head. She was not lying. It was the truth. She had brought her doctor along to prove it. . . . I prayed, 'God, if you can heal Judy, you can heal me; heal me to glorify your name' " (58).

KUHLMAN'S USE OF THE BIBLE

Like her predecessors in the faith, Kuhlman also relied heavily on scriptures to convince her followers to believe in the miraculous. This reliance should come as no surprise since her constituencies believed the Bible to be the inspired word of God, practically everything of which was directly relevant to their lives. Kuhlman simply perpetuated a belief system that most of her followers already accepted whenever she quoted or alluded to scripture regardless of what the scripture might say.

Kuhlman taught: "We need to get back to the word of God again. Know that if I teach you one thing and the word of God says another, the word is right. If your pastor says one thing and the Bible says another, the Bible is right. . . . And we've got to get back to the place where we take the word for the final authority." She then proceeded to preach on the miraculous healing of the lame man in Acts 3 as if what happened to him were normative for people today (*I Believe in Miracles* vol. III). Other passages that she often cited were Matthew 8:15–17 and James 5:14–15, among others (Warner 136; "I Believe in Miracles" 17).

Kuhlman believed—and explicitly taught others to believe—in the miraculous because she could read about it in the scriptures. "As I began studying the word," she disclosed, "I knew that divine healing was in the word of God and you cannot . . . study the word of God without knowing, without seeing that the healing for the physical, the healing for the whole man is in the word of God." Referring to Isaiah 53:5 ("By his stripes we are healed"), Kuhlman taught that individuals received both physical and spiritual healing as a result of Christ's crucifixion ("The Beginning of Miracles").

Although Kuhlman herself occasionally talked about the disappointment she experienced after witnessing the healing service in the tent of a post-World War II revivalist (she never disclosed the revivalist's name), she did not abandon her belief in miraculous healings. In spite of her disappointment she clung tenaciously to her belief that miracles were possible because she believed they were taught in the

Bible. According to her, although she "could not see scriptural heal-ing . . . I knew that whether or not I would ever see a miracle . . . it did not alter God's word one iota. I knew that if I'd lived and died and would never see a miracle . . . it still would not change God's word. God said it. He made provision for it" ("The Beginning of Miracles"). In effect Kuhlman was telling would-be skeptics that, even though they might not believe some physical demonstration, they should still believe that miraculous healings are possible simply be-cause the Bible, she believed, teaches they are possible.

Speaking before the Full Gospel Business Men's Fellowship Inter-national Convention in Dallas in 1973, Kuhlman warned how rhe-torically critical it was to use the Bible to convince people of the miraculous. "We've got to come back again to the Word of God. If we don't, we're going to lose the respect of the millions that are watching us and the thousands who are on the borderline waiting, watching, inside hungry, hungry" (Buckingham 44).

Suffice it to say that throughout her career as a faith healer, Kath-ryn Kuhlman attempted to persuade her followers to believe in mi-raculous healings by reminding them that the Bible supported them and that the miraculous still occurred in the twentieth century. "We have every right to have the same things happen in our churches this hour as happened on the Day of Pentecost [in Acts 2]," taught Kuhl-man ("The Beginning of Miracles"). This type of reasoning was probably rhetorically compelling because Kathryn's audiences—in the main—were not critical thinkers. They accepted everything that Kathryn quoted from the Bible as having a direct bearing on their lives. Kuhlman's scriptural allusions, whatever passage she cited, merely served to remind and reinforce her audiences of what they already believed.

KUHLMAN'S CONVERSION AND CALLING

As was pointed out earlier Kuhlman often told of her conversion and calling by God. She went to great lengths for audiences to know this, in large measure because she was a woman in a man's domain. Being a woman she often felt the need to justify why she was in the ministry. Nevertheless, the story of her conversion and calling was well-known to her followers.

She often dramatically relayed how she began to tremble during the altar call that Sunday morning while only fourteen years old in the small Methodist Church of Concordia, Missouri. In fact she shook so uncontrollably that she had to lay down her hymnal. Eventually, she made her way to the front of the building where she began to cry uncontrollably. "Something happened to Joe Kuhlman's girl," she disclosed. Kuhlman told of how this was her first "experience with the power of the Holy Spirit." "It was real to me, the most real thing to ever happen to me." "From that moment on, I had a great burden for souls" ("An Hour with Kathryn Kuhlman").

Although she believed she was the most unlikely person God could have chosen, Kuhlman nevertheless adamantly argued that her "call to the ministry was just as definite as my conversion" ("Baptism of the Holy Spirit"). "My call from him was . . . something I had to do" (*I Believe in Miracles* vol. I). "You can say anything you want about me, as a woman, having no right to stand in the pulpit and preach the gospel. Yet even if everybody in the world told me that, it would have no effect on me whatsoever. Why? Because my call to the ministry was just as definite as my conversion" (*A Glimpse into Glory* 11).

Lewis suggests that "special calling" is only one of many factors that play a role in the rhetorical success of a charismatic speaker. In Kuhlman's case, notes Lewis, "This supernatural call to the ministry and subsequently to a specific healing ministry gained adherents who saw in Miss Kuhlman the fulfillment of their desire for a symbolic leader who could be the mediator between God's healing power and their own diseased bodies" (230). Indeed, Kuhlman boosted her ethos and subsequent ability to persuade when she reminded her followers of her genuine conversion experience and ensuing call to preach. Audiences identified with Kuhlman's conversion experience because many, if not most, of them claimed to have had similar encounters with the Holy Spirit. Since they believed Kathryn's conversion story, they had no reason to doubt the report of her calling. And, if she were called by God, who were they to say otherwise?

Aside from what Kuhlman taught, other rhetorical factors, such as organization, style, and delivery are important. What effect did these factors have on her success as an evangelist and faith healer?

KUHLMAN'S ORGANIZATION

Lewis correctly points out that Kuhlman's sermons were not well organized. In fact, they did not appear to be organized at all. He describes them as " 'essay-like' ramblings" ("Charismatic Communication and Faith Healers" 219). Likewise, Warner calls her sermons "rambling lectures" (209). Buckingham points out that Maryon Marsh, close friend and office worker in Kathryn Kuhlman's foundation, thought that in later years of her ministry Kathryn's preaching was "desultory, repeating herself and meandering down well trodden paths" (145). Often Kuhlman would come on stage and tell her audiences that she intended to speak only for a few minutes. What began as a short talk wound up becoming an hour long, rambling discourse about whatever seemed to pop into her mind while she preached.

The fact that Kuhlman's lessons were not well organized should come as no surprise, however. With the exception of Oral Roberts, Kathryn's lack of organization was like the preaching of other twentieth-century faith healers. Indeed, she was true to form. Kathryn disclosed that she did not always know what she was going to say prior to going on stage. Instead, she trusted that the words would just come to her ("Charismatic Communication and Faith Healers" 219).

Kuhlman's lack of organization in no way impeded either her popularity or her persuasiveness. Frankly, her audiences were oblivious to her lack of organization. What Kuhlman had to say appeared to be more important to them than the order in which she said it. They were so engrossed in hearing about the miraculous that the order in which she presented ideas did not phase them. They were clearly more interested in substance than form.

KUHLMAN'S STYLE, DELIVERY, AND STAGE PRESENCE

"Pure corn" is the way Episcopalian priest and newspaper columnist Lester Kinsolving described Kuhlman's oratorical style in 1970 (Buckingham 75). Perhaps this was because of her slow, elongated speech. Speaking in what one of her biographers, Jamie Buckingham, describes as a "deep alto voice," Kuhlman often confessed, "I beeeeliEEEEVE in meeeericles." She often referred to Jesus as "JEEEZusss" and the Holy Spirit as "Hooooly Spir-it" (71, 172). "God" often became "Gawwwwd." Hart depicts her as having an "unusual" tone of voice and "a tendency to use vocal inflection almost to the point of overexaggeration when expressing solemnity, awe, joy, or displeasure" (60). She often began her radio broadcasts with, "Helloooo there. And have you been waiting for me?" During one radio program she began softly and slowly with, "Thissssss . . . is going to be ooooone of the most praaaaaatical heart . . . to . . . heart talks that you and I have ever had" ("The Beginning of Miracles").

In addition to her elongated pronunciation Kuhlman would often speak slowly and softly, even whispering to her audiences. Kuhlman was not always low keyed, however. Indeed she could and would often raise her voice, talking quite loudly and adamantly about a point. One could never mistake the urgency of her claims.

People reported that she possessed a "Cheshire cat grin, gleaming eyes, and voice that ranges from [an] intense hiss to extreme hushed tones of love as she talks about Jesus" (Farr 12). In short, when preaching she ran the gambit from slow and low to fast and loud depending on what mood she was in or how she wished to emphasize a point. Although arguably not possessing as dramatic a stage presence as her female predecessor Aimee Semple McPherson, Kuhlman was also an entertainer. Red-headed, very thin, and almost six feet tall in her high heels, she frequently would walk briskly to the center of the stage in a long, flowing, tight-waisted white gown with puffy sleeves that covered outstretched arms. *Time* once referred to her as "diminutive," "middle-class, fiftyish, a lady who likes fine clothes" and "wears a 1945 Shirley Temple hairdo" ("Miracle Woman" 62). Helen Hosier, one of Kuhlman's biographers, suggests that Kathryn "always dressed beautifully, often in a flowing gown of a soft, chiffonlike fabric that draped about her lovely swirling folds" (95).

Describing her delivery Speed suggests she was a "striking figure" and "energetic minister" who "appeared to be in constant motion and displayed a wide range of dramatic moods and voices" (n. pag.). Myra White, who ran Kuhlman's Hollywood Office disclosed, "When I first saw her, I didn't know what to think . . . what is this? She's very dramatic, you know, dancing all over the place" (Farr 12). Writing in *Coronet* magazine, Cooke said of Kuhlman, "Her oratory skill is an interesting combination of dramatics, humor, and humanness" (Hosier 95).

Occasionally upon entering the stage, Kuhlman would march to the center, turn toward one side or the other, pirouette backward on her tiptoes with her hands raised high above her head toward her audience as if to say, "Thank you for coming" (*Dry Land, Living Waters*). The *New York Times* once said of her, "Almost glamorous in a gold-collar white sheath dress with her rust-colored hair, the evangelist would extend her arm skyward, close her eyes and then reveal a healing in progress" ("Kathryn Kuhlman . . . Dies in Tulsa" 48). To the uninitiated, Kuhlman's style, delivery, and stage presence probably looked and sounded bizarre, but to her followers, who were used to her mannerisms, these behaviors were normal.

CONCLUSION

Kathryn Kuhlman was a rhetorically successful faith healer as judged by the millions who flocked to churches and convention halls during her lifetime to hear her preach, catch a glimpse of a healing, or perhaps, even to experience one themselves. Like other healing revivalists who practiced before her, she seemed to understand what it took to convince those in attendance of the miraculous. She employed examples and testimonies, she evoked the Bible, she reminded audiences time and time again of her special calling, she gave God the credit while simultaneously deprecating herself—all of this in an attempt to offer hope to many who had all but given up hope. Additionally, Kuhlman's followers lapped up her ecumenicalism and excellent sense of humor packaged in a highly conversational, sometimes homespun, yet always entertaining (if not a little bizarre) style. Indeed she had her finger on the pulse of mass persuasion. She seemed to know intuitively what her audiences liked and she gave it to them.

Perhaps she learned some of her rhetorical skills by watching other faith healers such as Aimee Semple McPherson. Warner points out that Kuhlman probably audited classes at Aimee Semple McPherson's L.I.F.E. Bible college and attended McPherson's services at Angelus Temple as a young woman (35). Maybe Kuhlman learned *most* of her techniques by watching others. Who is to say? Nevertheless, she had a way of endearing herself to her followers. Her influence would be felt even after her death through Benny Hinn, even though the two never personally met one another. He is the subject of the next chapter.

For many individuals who believed in Kathryn Kuhlman, perhaps Buckingham's assessment of her is as accurate as any in pointing out why she was so appealing: "At sixty she was the perfect combination of sex, showmanship, spirituality, and a domineering mother" (Buckingham 53).

Since her death in 1976 the twentieth century has yet to see another woman as influential and rhetorically successful as was the red-haired "preacher lady" from Concordia, Missouri (Neal 28).

REFERENCES

Buckingham, Jamie. *Daughter of Destiny*. Plainfield, NJ: Logos International, 1976.

Farr, Louise. "The Divine Ms. K." *People* Jan. 1975: 12–15.

God's Generals. Vol. 7 (Parts I and II). Narr. Roberts Liardon. Tulsa, OK: Infinity Video, 1988.

Hart, Alberta Sophia. "Kathryn Kuhlman: An Analysis of Communicative Ritual in the Great Miracle Service." Thesis. California State University, 1974.

"Healing in the Spirit: Kathryn Kuhlman." *Christianity Today* 20 July 1973: 4–10.

Hosier, Helen Kooiman. *Kathryn Kuhlman: The Life She Led, The Legacy She Left*. Old Tappan, NJ: Fleming H. Revell Co., 1976.

"Kathryn Kuhlman, Evangelist and Faith Healer, Dies in Tulsa." *New York Times* 22 Feb. 1976: 48.

"Kathryn Kuhlman: To God Be the Glory." *Acts* (Mar.–Apr. 1976): 7–12.

Kuhlman, Kathryn. "Baptism of the Holy Spirit." Audiocassette, n.d.

———. "The Beginning of Miracles." Audiocassette, 1972.

———. *Dry Land, Living Waters: Las Vegas Miracle Service*. Prod. and Dir. Dick Ross. Videocassette, 1975.

———. *A Glimpse into Glory*. Plainfield, NJ: Logos International, 1979.

———. *God Can Do It Again*. 1969. South Plainfield, NJ: Bridge Publishing, Inc., 1993.

———. "An Hour with Kathryn Kuhlman." Audiocassette, n.d.

———. *I Believe in Miracles*. Englewood Cliffs, NJ: Prentice-Hall, Inc., 1962.

———. "I Believe in Miracles." Radio Sermon, n.d.

———. *I Believe in Miracles*. Vol. I–III. Videocassette, 1995.

———. "In Tribute to Kathryn Kuhlman." Audiocassette, n.d.

———. *Never Too Late*. South Plainfield, NJ: Bridge Publishing, Inc., 1975.

———. "Why Aren't Some Healed? (no. 1 and no. 2)." Radio Sermon, n.d.

Lairdon, Roberts. *Kathryn Kuhlman: A Spiritual Biography of God's Miracle Working Power*. Tulsa, OK: Harrison House, 1990.

Lanning, Gwen. *Twilight and Dawn*. South Plainfield, NJ: Bridge Publishing Inc., 1976.

"The Late Kathryn Kuhlman: Truly a Worker of God." *National Courier* 19 Mar. 1976: n.p.

Lewis, Todd V. "Charismatic Communication and Faith Healers." Diss. Louisiana State University, 1980.

McDonald, Jimmie. *The Kathryn Kuhlman I Knew*. Shippensburg, PA: Treasure House, 1996.

"Miracle Woman." *Time* 14 Sept. 1970: 62, 64.

Neal, Emily Gardner. "Can Faith in God Heal the Sick?" *Redbook* Nov. 1950: 28–31, 93–96.

Nolen, William A. *Healing: A Doctor in Search of a Miracle*. New York: Random House, 1974.

Speed, Billie Cheney. "Woman Evangelist Draws 8,000 Here." *Atlanta Journal* 5 Oct. 1973: n.p.

Warner, Wayne E. *Kathryn Kuhlman: The Woman Behind the Miracles*. Ann Arbor, MI: Servant Publications, 1993.

CHAPTER SEVEN

They Call Him "Pastor": Benny Hinn

It was 6:30 on an October Thursday evening in Nashville, Tennessee. The year was 1997. A young man stepped to a microphone of the Nashville Arena and welcomed the audience: "Turn to your neighbor and say, 'Something good is going to happen tonight.'" Excitement filled the air. After five minutes of introductory remarks about "Pastor Benny Hinn," the young man directed over 20,000 people's attention to the jumbo monitor hanging in the middle of the arena. Suddenly the screen lit up with a video explaining the mission of Benny Hinn Media Ministries and inviting individuals to become Covenant Partners. The show of one of the most popular contemporary faith healers had begun.

HINN'S BACKGROUND

Called by some a "flamboyant fraud" and by others a "modern-day faith healer" (Midday Newscast) and "spiritual superstar" ("Impact"), Benny Hinn was born Palestinian on December 3, 1952, in Jaffa, Israel (present-day Tel Aviv) to Clemence and Costandi Hinn. The second of eight children, six of which were boys, Benny was named after Benedictus, the Greek Orthodox patriarch of Jerusalem

Evangelist Benny Hinn waves to the faithful at the Charlotte Coliseum, Charlotte, NC, September 25, 1995. Photographer: Bob Leverone. Reprinted with permission of *The Charlotte Observer*.

who christened him as an infant. Hinn's mother Clemence was Armenian. His father Costandi was Greek. According to Hinn—although scholars question him on this point—his father was mayor of his home town Jaffa during much of his childhood. In reality Hinn's father was "a clerk in an Arab labor office." When questioned, Hinn claimed that his father performed the duties of a mayor (Frame 54; Davis D7).

At the age of two, Hinn's parents enrolled him in a Catholic preschool where he would spend the next twelve years of his life being educated by nuns and monks. Although he attended the Greek Orthodox church with his parents on Sundays, the rest of the week he studied Catholicism and celebrated Mass. Benny records, "Was I Catholic? Absolutely. Catholicism was my prayer life. It occupied my time and attention five days a week. It became my mentality. . . . I was an expert on the Catholic life" (Hinn 17–21).

In spite of the fact that "virtually no spirituality accompanied" what he was taught in the Catholic schools he attended, Hinn reveals how grateful he was to have received such a thorough teaching of the Bible at such an early age from the monks and nuns. He claims he was also fortunate to have grown up in Israel, where school field trips "literally made God's Word come to life" (Hinn 16–21).

As a boy, Hinn claims to have been "extremely religious." "I prayed and I prayed—probably more than some Christians pray today. But all I knew how to pray was the Hail Mary, the Creed, the Lord's Prayer, and other prescribed prayers." He recalls how the first of many supernatural visions in his life occurred to him when he was only eleven. According to Hinn, Jesus walked into his bedroom and smiled at him without saying a word. He was asleep when his "little body was caught up in an incredible sensation that can only be described as 'electric.' It felt as if someone had plugged me into a wired socket. There was a numbness that felt like needles—a million of them—rushing through my body." Insisting that it was no dream, Hinn believes that God allowed him "to experience a vision that would create an indelible impression on my young life" (Hinn 21–22).

Aside from being religious as a child, Hinn also claims to have had a stuttering problem that took its toll on his self-esteem, although critics challenge Hinn on this point as well, citing individuals who knew Hinn as a boy but knew nothing of his stuttering (Frame 54). Nevertheless, according to Benny, "My own self-image was practically destroyed because of my speech impediment." Such "stammering" was often set off by the "smallest amount of social pressure or nervousness." The isolation and ridicule that it brought him was "almost unbearable" (Hinn 10, 21).

Political tensions mounted in Hinn's homeland in the early 1960s. Within months after the Six-Day War eventually erupted on June 5, 1967, between Israel and its Arab neighbors Egypt, Jordan, and Syria, Hinn's father gathered the family together and informed them that he planned to move them to Canada. In July 1968 the Hinns immigrated to Toronto where they would be safe from fighting and terrorism in the Middle East. Although Benny claims to have been fourteen when he left his native Jaffa in July 1968, in actuality he would have been closer to sixteen.

In Toronto Hinn dropped out of Georges Vanier Secondary School, but not before being introduced to the Jesus Movement and the concept of being "born again." This introduction came from high school classmates whom Hinn considered fanatical. Hinn tells of how he would go out of his way to avoid this "bunch of weirdos" who constantly tried to "witness" to him (Hinn 26–28; "Impact").

Although some of the details of this story—like other stories Hinn tells—are in dispute (Frame 54), according to Hinn during his senior year on a cold night in February 1972, he claims to have experienced another vision while in his bedroom. Among other things he saw an angel which "hovered just ahead of me, just a few steps away." The angel led him through a doorway and "into the light" before taking him by the hand and dropping him on Don Mills Road, at the corner of his high school.

The next morning Hinn hurried to school to study before classes began. While reading in the school's library several of his "crazy" friends walked over to his table and invited him to a morning prayer meeting in a room adjacent to the library. While in the devotional Hinn prayed out loud, "Lord Jesus, come back." For the rest of the day, he recalls seeing the face of Jesus and "wiping the tears from my eyes." "And the only thing I could say was, "Jesus, I love you. . . . Jesus, I love you" (Hinn 28–32).

Benny claims to have begun an intense period of Bible study shortly thereafter in which he contends he was taught by the Holy Spirit. He began attending weekly fellowship meetings with his fanatical friends in "The Catacombs" of St. Paul's Cathedral, a downtown Toronto

Anglican Church. It was during one of these meetings that Hinn "made a public confession of his acceptance of Christ."

While suffering severe persecution and ostracism by his family—particularly from his father—Hinn's urge to preach began to boil within him. After disclosing to a friend his visions and recent experiences, he was invited to give the same testimony to the church where his friend was a member. On December 7, 1974, at the age of twenty-two, Hinn stood in the pulpit of Trinity Assembly of God in Oshawa, Canada about thirty miles east of Toronto. To a group of about one hundred people, Hinn delivered his first sermon which consisted largely of his personal testimony.

It was also on this night that Hinn claims to have received a miracle. According to Benny, the moment he opened his mouth to preach God cured him of his stuttering. "When God healed me, the healing was permanent" (Hinn 34–47).

In 1975, feeling led by the Holy Spirit, Hinn began holding weekly meetings in Toronto on Monday evenings. After meeting in a high school auditorium he eventually moved to "larger facilities" where "hundreds and hundreds of people attended." These meetings were marked by "healing lines" and "testimonies of miracles." Like Kathryn Kuhlman's services people claimed to be healed while merely sitting in their seats (Hinn 163–64).

After being invited to Orlando, Florida to preach in July 1978 at the church of Roy Harthern, a prominent Orlando minister, Hinn moved from Toronto to Orlando in 1979, the same year he married Harthern's daughter Suzanne. Eventually they would have four children together, three daughters and a son.

According to Benny, the Holy Spirit told him in 1977 while he was riding in a Yellow Cab in Pittsburgh "to build a church and establish an international ministry." Hinn believed that God led him to Orlando from where he would launch his ministry. Four years later in 1983, Benny began the Orlando Christian Center "with just a handful of people." According to him, today "it touches the lives of thousands of people every week, plus a national television audience" with his daily, thirty-minute program "This Is Your Day," which is taped at Hinn's World Media Center in Aliso Viejo, California. According to Paul Crouch of Trinity Broadcast Network, "This Is Your Day" is carried over ten satellites worldwide, reaching into Russia, Africa, Europe, the Mediterranean, and North and South America.

Benny Hinn Media Ministries has targeted India and China. In the United States alone his program is carried on more than ninety television stations and cable companies (Hinn 165–66; Observation by author, Oct. 1997; "Covenant Partners in Ministry"). In 1997 Benny Hinn Media Ministries grossed over $60,000,000, almost twice the amount of 1995 ("Impact").

In addition to his television program Hinn has authored three best-selling books. Two of his most popular are *Good Morning, Holy Spirit* and *The Anointing*, which, according to *Christianity Today*, by 1992 had sold a combined total of 1.7 million copies (Frame 52). As of 1997 Hinn's organization claims that *Good Morning, Holy Spirit, The Anointing*, and *Welcome, Holy Spirit* have sold more than four million copies ("Ministry Profile").

In 1990 Hinn began holding crusades both in and out of the United States. According to David Palmquist, one of Hinn's associate pastors, "Pastor Benny" travels over 200 days a year in crusades but "seeing a person get out of a wheelchair never gets old." It was the 1997 Nashville Crusade where, according to Benny, "the power of God was so amazing," that set the backdrop for the current analysis ("Miracles from Singapore" Nov. 12, 1997).

THE 1997 NASHVILLE CRUSADE

Around 6:45 p.m. a professional band, composed of drums, bass guitar, and keyboard struck up a medley of tunes with a strong back-beat. The audience began to clap in unison. Behind the band sat a thousand-member, locally volunteered choir, men in white shirts and variously colored neckties, women in royal or navy blue dresses. As music filled the air people of all races and ages continued to take their seats, arms filled with refreshments from the concession stands. Seeing this alone, one could easily have mistaken the scene for a sporting event.

Those in attendance appeared to come from all walks of life— Asian, Latino, African-Americans, and Caucasian; rich, poor, and middle class, but mainly middle class. A minority of men wore coats, ties, and three-piece suits. Here and there, women were adorned in dresses and high heels with stockings. Mostly, though, people wore blue jeans, tee shirts, sweat shirts, flannel shirts, and tennis or other casual shoes. Clearly, these were ordinary, everyday people who had turned out to see a miracle, or more importantly, to receive one themselves.

Over to the right a young girl with drawn up hands continued clapping in unison—as best she could. Like others scattered throughout the arena she then raised her hands above her head in praise, with eyes fast closed, mouthing, "Thank you Jesus, Thank you Jesus." On the arena floor below sat people in wheelchairs, some elderly with no apparent ailment, others—both young and old alike—contorted and drooling. Some sat hooked to oxygen tanks. Like so many throughout this century who have attended meetings of previous healing revivalists, no doubt they turned out this evening, hoping for a miracle to free them from the shackles of their affliction. For most, however, this night it was not to be.

Around 7:10, approximately twenty guest ministers—primarily pastors of sponsoring local churches—took their seats on the right side of the platform. Among the guests were Ralph Wilkerson from Melodyland Christian Center in Anaheim, California and Steve Summerall, son of Lester Summerall. The next evening would bring Jan and Paul Crouch of the famed Trinity Broadcasting Network, as well as the Minister of Tourism from the Middle East country of Jordan. Spotlights panned the audience as Bruce Hughes, a classically trained pianist, tickled the ivory of his black Baldwin grand piano. Cameras on booms or on shoulders of cameramen roaming the stage filmed his artistry which was relayed to the jumbo monitor above. One could not help but think how far healing revivalism had come from the sawdust days of the 1940s and 1950s. Indeed, compared to the resources of William Branham and Oral Roberts, the display this night was high-tech wizardry.

After Hughes completed his performance, Alvin Slaughter, a black male who looks more like a linebacker in the National Football League than a gospel singer, stepped forward and belted out a jazzed-up version of "Oh Lord, How Majestic Is Your Name in All the Earth," a song made popular by contemporary Christian artist Sandi Patti. By this point the standing crowd was rocking as the music blared and Alvin screamed into the microphone. The noise was deafening. When Alvin concluded the audience settled—but only momentarily. Then the choir quickly struck up an upbeat version of "Nothing is Impossible with God," followed by "He Touched Me," and "How Great Thou Art." The entire assembly stood and raised their hands in praise. The scene had been set for the main attraction of the evening—Benny Hinn himself.

While the choir and audience sang "How Great Thou Art," Hinn made his way to center stage. Shorter than most men, Benny has an olive complexion and a thick mixture of gray and black hair parted on the right, extending to his collar. This night, as on many other nights, he wore an off-white, double-breasted suit with white shirt, red tie, and matching red handkerchief neatly placed in his coat pocket. A gold watchband and diamond ring adorned his wrist and hand. *Publisher's Weekly* describes Hinn as "impeccably dressed and smooth-as-silk. . . . He looks more like a Man Who Has Arrived, straight off the pages of GQ, than a simple Southern preacher" (Bearden 42).

"Are you ready for one of the greatest crusades you've ever had?" he screamed to his audience. "Yes!" came back an excited reply. After a few words to his audience about his previous crusade in Miami, Hinn introduced two soloists, one after the other, who sang for the crowd. By now, the audience was totally engulfed in the electric atmosphere.

When the soloists finished Hinn began talking in a conversational tone about upcoming events and things that happened in past crusades, namely various miracles. He then proceeded to take up an offering. Here Hinn's persuasive skills emerged in full bloom. Before asking everyone to make out their checks "in English and not in tongues" to Benny Hinn Media Ministries or not to forget their number and expiration date on their Visa or Mastercard, he told of how he once was in debt and "not a giver." After being chastised by his father-in-law, he began to "tithe." In time, he paid off his debts. Hinn related how his father-in-law taught him that "if you pay God's bills, He'll pay yours." The implication was that if those in attendance donated money to Benny Hinn, God would multiply their investment back to them. A woman sitting next to this author proceeded to write a check for thirty dollars. While the ushers passed the buckets for people to drop in their contributions, Bruce Hughes played the piano "to say thank you."

Not long after the collection, shortly after nine o'clock in the evening, Hinn launched into what might be called a sermon. Actually, it appeared to resemble what he had been doing prior to taking up the offering—just talking to the audience about whatever came into his mind. The difference in the two, however, lay in the fact that the second talk began by asking the audience to turn to Psalms 86, marking this phase as the "sermon" stage of the revival. Pages began rattling all over the auditorium as the audience prepared to follow Hinn's reading. Hinn spent the next fifty minutes justifying from the Bible why people should believe in miracles.

Around ten o'clock he began to conclude his talk. With the organ, piano, and band playing in the background and the choir singing, Hinn announced, "My Friend, he's about to come into this auditorium. There's something happening." The music crescendoed. As the choir sang, "Rise and be healed in the name of Jesus," Hinn sang along with them. By now the audience was on their feet, hands lifted in praise all over the auditorium, totally engulfed in the atmosphere. Then Hinn yelled to the hypnotized crowd, "All you have to do is lift your hand, lift your faith." Once again the noise of the music mixed with Hinn's voice was deafening. As the choir transitioned to "He touched Me," ushers frantically rolled wheelchairs to the front of the auditorium.

Shortly the noise abated. The house became relatively quiet while the choir softly transitioned to "Alleluia," changing keys a second or third time through it. "Sing it, choir," Hinn admonished. He then turned and stood facing the audience with the microphone in his raised right hand, with eyes fast closed. "Miracles are happening here," he quickly announced. "You devil of disease, sin, and sickness . . . in Jesus' name, I order you to let them go; let them go."

He then turned to his left and announced that someone was being healed of "arthritis," "cancer," "bone cancer," "diabetes," "eye problems," "skin condition." He yelled that someone's left leg was being healed. "Someone with a spinal injury" and "a heart condition" was being healed. "An ear drum is being healed." "Cancer of the liver, come out! Come out, I say!" "Alice has just been healed of deep depression." "A brain tumor is being healed." "A neck injury is being healed." "A bleeding ulcer is being healed." "Many of you feel like fire [is] upon you, like electricity [is] upon you."

After announcing these miracles, Hinn asked those healed to line up to the left or right of the stage so that they could come forward to give their testimony. Long lines began to jam the aisles to the right and left of the stage. As the music grew faster and louder, in break-neck speed, ushers began lining the stage with walkers, wheelchairs, oxygen tanks, and crutches. The audience had been whipped into a frenzy. It all appeared to be carefully orchestrated. "Look at this," exclaimed Benny, "We have a traffic jam on the platform." "I've never seen as many empty wheelchairs on the first night as I've seen in Nashville, Tennessee," he boasted. As if someone had just scored a touchdown, the audience erupted in applause and praise.

Assistant Steve Brock on one end of the platform and assistant Joan Geesen on the other end dramatically introduced those who had lined up on stage to claim their miracle. With a sense of urgency in her voice, Joan frantically and loudly announced to the arena, "Pastor Hinn, this woman has had diabetes for forty years and her husband here says he has never seen her out of her wheelchair prior to tonight!" The audience exploded with gasps and applause. When queried by Hinn, however, the man and the woman revealed that they had been married only for a few years. When Joan initially introduced the lady, the audience was led to believe that the husband and wife had been married for the full forty years. The audience naturally thought that it had actually been that long since the husband had seen his wife walk.

A little girl and her mother made their way to the stage this evening. The child was supposedly deaf in one ear and blind in her right eye but now could see and hear as a result of a miracle she received. After the mother was "slain in the spirit"—at which point she fell backward into the arms of waiting ushers—Hinn proceeded to talk to the little girl. Then turning to the audience he quipped, "I wonder what the devil is doing now. I think he just had a massive heart attack." The audience roared with laughter.

After slaying in the spirit a self-proclaimed arm wrestling champion Hinn boasted, "Who does the devil think he is?" The frenzied audience clapped, waved, screamed, gasped, and laughed over one miracle after another. The atmosphere was electric; the noise was deafening. This night God's servant could do no wrong.

Another little girl, who was "born deaf" but healed moments earlier, came to the stage. Hinn tried to talk to her, but the little girl had difficulty repeating the words that Benny asked her to repeat. Coming to Hinn's rescue, Joan reminded the audience, "Pastor, she hasn't been able to hear since birth so she hasn't learned to speak as well as she should." This seemed to be an adequate explanation for those looking on as they began to laugh and applaud in agreement.

Of all of the cases of healing this evening, perhaps the one most difficult for the uninitiated to understand occurred when Hinn cast out the demon of a woman with leukemia. While the woman lay on the ground in a contorted position, Hinn yelled, "You devil of cancer, leave this woman." After a few moments the ushers lifted the woman to her feet, her bald head shining in the spotlight as she held her wig that had fallen off in her right hand. Hinn proceeded to tell her that, while she lay on the ground, "a serpent came out" of her left foot and slithered across the stage. Hinn saw it with his own eyes he assured the audience. The woman corroborated his story when she told him that she felt the serpent leave her foot. Once again, the audience approvingly erupted in applause.

The most bizarre event was yet to come. After over an hour of healings and testimonies Hinn had all non-musical personnel leave the platform so that they "won't go flying" from the power of the Holy Spirit. He then turned around and yelled "touch" at the top of his voice, at which point the entire choir fell backward as they were slain in the spirit. He then turned to the audience to his right. "Do you want it?" he screamed. "Yes!" came back the reply in unison. Then, after pausing for ten or fifteen seconds—long enough for the audience to grow quiet—Hinn quickly yelled "touch" at the top of his lungs. The startled section fell backward to Hinn's ear-piercing command. In rapid fire succession, he proceeded to scream "touch, touch, touch" and three more sections of people fell backward.

By this point it was well past 11:00 p.m. The night had been spent. Diseases had been healed. Demons had been cast out. Thousands had been slain in the spirit. People were made to feel better. And there was nothing more for Hinn to do except make a few announcements about the next evening's meeting and bid everyone a good night as the choir sang "Battle Hymn of the Republic."

It was clear to this author that Hinn had cast a rhetorical spell on well over 20,000 people this evening. Even charismatic theologian J. Rodman Williams of Regent University admits that Hinn often mixes "psychological techniques . . . with the spiritual" (Frame 54). A close look at his *modus operandi* suggests that Hinn employs many of the same persuasive strategies—consciously or unconsciously—as did many of his forerunners in the twentieth century.

HINN'S HUMILITY

One of the first rhetorical inventions to leave Hinn's lips when he arrives on stage is to remind his audience why they are there. He does this in his opening prayer. "I will give you the glory and the honor for every miracle," Hinn prayed to God. "The people have not come to see me. They've come to see you. The people have not come to hear me but to hear you." During his Friday evening service in his Nashville crusade, Benny opened in a similar fashion when he prayed, "We vow . . . we will give you the praise." "They've not come to see me, to hear me; they've come to praise you." Hinn is quick to remind others, "I don't heal anybody. The Lord is the healer" ("Impact").

Turning to a nearby gentleman prior to the start of the Friday night crusade, this author asked him what he admired about Benny Hinn. The man responded, "I like the joy in his eyes, the scriptural references, and the fact that he takes no credit for the miracles." Clearly, as is the case with other faith healers throughout the twentieth century, Hinn knows that giving God the glory goes a long way toward endearing himself to those in attendance. Hinn's rhetoric is like his idol Kathryn Kuhlman or any other faith healer of the twentieth century in this regard.

HINN AND SCRIPTURE

Just as the above man in attendance intimated, Benny Hinn uses a plethora of scripture. These references become rhetorically compelling in selling the notion of faith healing due largely to the fact that most of those in attendance are Pentecostal or charismatic as judged by the response Hinn received when he asked, "How many in attendance are Catholic?" "How many in attendance are Baptist?" "How many here are Pentecostal?"

Since Pentecostals and charismatics believe, as do many other protestant conservatives, that the Bible is the final say on matters of religion, if Hinn can at least give the impression that he is grounding his teachings in the scriptures, then he has essentially won over his audience regardless of what they might see with their eyes. Any other rhetorical techniques beyond that merely reinforce what he teaches. So, when he uses a multiplicity of verses to teach that miraculous physical healing should accompany salvation or spiritual healing—no matter how out of context they may appear to those who scrutinize what he says—he establishes not only the possibility but the definitiveness of miraculous cures in the minds of his Pentecostal and charismatic hearers. In attempting to justify Benny Hinn's on-stage antics to the media, Rick Nash, a spokesperson for Benny Hinn, argues that what he does is "described in the Bible," that Benny Hinn is only doing "what the scriptures teach" (Midday Newscast).

Among the many verses that Hinn used during his Nashville crusade were Psalms 103: 2–3, the gist of which states that God heals diseases. Hinn takes this verse literally. "God does not lie." "He cannot change what he said in His word." "The word of God does not say He heals some of thy diseases . . . but all of thy diseases." After citing Psalms 34:19, which states that Jehovah delivers the righteous from afflictions, Hinn assured his listeners, "You can walk out of here perfectly whole." "God has guaranteed to heal all thy diseases" "if you'll believe his word."

At this point Hinn began to reason by analogy. He reminded his audience that they believe in a doctor's prescription even though "we can't read it." Just as individuals have faith in the doctor and the label on the bottle of medicine, so should they have faith "in God's promise" as "you do in that little label," even though people don't understand "the little label on the bottle." "All you have to do is follow directions." After citing James 1:6–7, Hinn pointed out that "the word of God declares, 'Ask in faith, nothing wavering.' " To him, like most other faith healers, faith is a prerequisite to receiving and keeping a miraculous cure.

Even though this night Hinn did not explicitly quote Hebrews 13: 8 as have other healers in the twentieth century, he was quick to point out that God "cannot change." "He's the same Jesus 2,000 years ago as he is today." Hinn went on to cite Isaiah 53:5, which suggests "with his stripes we are healed." "If salvation is for all, healing is for all." "God includes physical healing as well as spiritual healing."

One of Hinn's final scriptural references this night was Matthew 9, which narrates the story about a woman with "an issue of blood" who was healed. Although Matthew's account does not name the woman, Hinn called her Lydia. Relying heavily on pathos as the organ played softly in the background to create the proper mood, Hinn relayed how this woman had an "incurable disease," yet Jesus healed her. "Her bleeding, frail, dusty hand touched him [Jesus]," suggested Hinn. Hinn relayed how the woman looked up at Jesus "with dust in her hair" and "bleeding hands." The scriptural reference and the emotion with which Hinn conveyed it, served to cap off a sermon packed full of proof texts used to convince his gullible audience.

TESTIMONIES, ARTIFACTS, AND EMPIRICAL DEMONSTRATIONS

As the case with other faith healers throughout this book, Hinn relies heavily upon the testimony of those who have been healed to convince others. One bald-headed boy, for example, named Shawn came to the platform and claimed to have been healed of leukemia. He told of how he was "nauseous" and "feeling bad" but started to feel good enough to stand up. The audience accepted this as proof of a miraculous cure by applauding him.

Another boy from Georgia named Joseph testified to having over 250 tumors disappear while sitting in the audience. With music blasting in the background, Hinn pulled Shawn and Joseph together on stage and prayed over them that God would "put them in the ministry" before slaying each of them in the spirit. After all was said and done, there was hardly a dry eye in the house. The audience approved with applause, reinforced with "praise God" and "praise the Lord."

On occasion Hinn will introduce an individual to the audience who had been healed in a former crusade. During the Thursday night of his Nashville crusade, Hinn did just this, asking the son of a Baptist preacher who had been healed of a brain tumor in a Little Rock, Arkansas crusade to stand. After reminding the audience that doctors had given up hope before God healed the man, Hinn pointed out that now doctors cannot find a "sign" of the tumor. The implication, of course, is that if a doctor cannot find evidence of sickness, then the individual must have been healed by God. Relying on the testimony of doctors, then, becomes another convincing factor in inducing audiences to believe in the miraculous.

During the sermon on the Friday night of his Nashville crusade, Hinn reminded the audience of how he himself spent three days in a hospital with a "bleeding valve" in his heart in 1985 and how God has healed him to the point that "God has even kept my teeth from cavities." These kinds of personal anecdotes, along with the story of how God supposedly healed him of stuttering suggest to those who are not sure about miracles that Hinn knows what he is talking about because he himself has personally experienced them.

Whether it is an individual giving his own testimony, Joan or Steve dramatically telling the story of a person's cure, or Hinn himself telling about either his own or someone else's healing, testimony plays an integral role in the persuasion process of Benny Hinn just as it has across the twentieth century.

Not only would Hinn have individuals testify to the audience, but he would also have them demonstrate their healings physically. Whether having people walk or run across the stage or bend and stretch, Hinn wanted his audience to see with their own eyes how well off people were now. According to Hinn, all one had to do to believe in miracles is to see how active on stage people were. The problem for skeptics, however, is the fact that the audience really is not privy to how physically disabled a person was to begin with. Those looking on are often led to believe that many people claiming healings were in worse physical condition than they actually were.

Frankly, many physical demonstrations were disappointing to this author. As was noted earlier, for example, people who were supposedly healed of deafness did not appear to hear Hinn at all when asked to repeat his words. Moreover, they certainly were not able to articulate clearly when asked to speak. Ironically and inexplainably, audiences still gasped and applauded as if they believed in spite of the evidence. Honest observers are forced to ask, where is the miracle? Yet, Hinn's audience, almost on cue, applauded or nodded in approval offering positive feedback and propelling along the healing circus.

All of these demonstrations were conducted in a musically noisy, electric atmosphere with nonverbal symbols plainly in view. The wheelchairs, crutches, and oxygen tanks that lined the front of the stage were overt signs to those in attendance that great miracles had been wrought this evening. Like Kathryn Kuhlman who lined her stages with wheelchairs, like Aimee Semple McPherson who displayed wheelchairs, crutches, and braces in glass cases at Angelus Temple, and like the post World War II healer Jack Coe who lined the top of his tents with canes, crutches, and braces, Hinn seemed to understand the visual impact that these artifacts would have on those in attendance. Certainly they were in plain view for everyone to see. The ushers had made sure of this.

IN THE KATHRYN KUHLMAN TRADITION

Those who follow Benny Hinn realize the profound influence that Kathryn Kuhlman had on his personal life and ministry even though the two never personally met. He tells of how, in 1973, he first sat through one of the tall redhead's services at the First Presbyterian Church in downtown Pittsburgh. According to Hinn, as he sat in the third row listening to Kuhlman speak, he felt overcome by the Holy Spirit. And at one point in her sermon, she pointed her long, bony finger at Hinn and said, " 'He's [Holy Spirit] more real than anything in this world!' " (Hinn 2–10).

Feeling puzzled on his bus trip back to Toronto, Hinn continually pondered what Kuhlman meant. He discloses how he wanted what Kathryn Kuhlman had. While praying in his room Hinn recounts he uttered these words, which are well-known to those who follow him: "Holy Spirit. Kathryn Kuhlman says you are her friend. . . . I don't think I know you. . . . Can I meet you?" (Hinn 12).

As part of his rhetorical appeal Hinn tells a version of this story to crusade audiences. He told his Nashville followers, for example, of how he received "an anointing" that Sunday morning in the First Presbyterian Church in 1973 while visiting a Kathryn Kuhlman service. Hinn boasts that "demons cannot touch me because I wear the anointing on my garment." When discussing his "spiritual heritage" to the Nashville crowd, he proclaimed, "I go back to Kathryn Kuhlman." "God revealed to me my spiritual heritage." "Kathryn influenced my life." "A lot of preachers bless me," disclosed Hinn, "but only one brings back my life and that's Kathryn Kuhlman." Critic Ole Anthony suggests that Hinn has gone so far that he has "aped all of Kathryn Kuhlman's mannerisms." The only difference in the two, suggests Anthony, is that Kathryn Kuhlman wore a white dress while Benny Hinn wears a white suit ("Impact"). What is ironic about this whole discussion is that Hinn never even met Kuhlman personally, according to the Kathryn Kuhlman Foundation (Gray). Although the two never communicated, Hinn leaves the impression that he and Kuhlman were the best of friends when she was alive.

Not only did Hinn align himself with Kathryn Kuhlman, but he also claimed to be a part of a long line of healing revivalists that can be traced all the way back to Maria Woodworth-Etter, who began her long, illustrious career as a healing revivalist in the late eighteenth century. Since Aimee Semple McPherson was influenced by Maria Woodworth-Etter, and since Kathryn Kuhlman was influenced by Aimee Semple McPherson, Hinn claimed to belong in the same "stream" of "healing revivalists." "We belong in the same lot," boasted Hinn. He went on to admonish the audience to "be careful who your father is in the spirit. Be careful who you're connected to. Thank God for Kathryn."

To add to his credibility Hinn also told his Nashville audience that while riding one night in 1978 in Pittsburgh with Marguerite "Maggie" Hartner, Kathryn Kuhlman's closest friend and confidante, she told him that God was going to give him a greater anointing than God gave Kathryn Kuhlman. After telling him at a stop light that he had more anointing than Kathryn had upon her at his age, Maggie disclosed, "If God can only trust you, he'll give you a lot more anointing than she had."

When Hinn tells his audiences that he comes from a long line of healing revivalists and that he has a greater anointing than Kathryn Kuhlman, he realizes that he is boosting his credibility. Instead of guilt by association, Hinn is creating glory by association, for his audiences realize who these venerable female forerunners were and hold them in high esteem. If they had been blessed by God, then he is too, because he supposedly comes from the same tradition. If individuals place stock in Maggie Hartner's remarks, then they may believe that Benny Hinn's ministry is even greater than that of Kuhlman's.

So, what an audience witnesses when they attend a Benny Hinn crusade should be given credence because he is merely a continuation in a long line of healing revivalists. In this way he contributes to the selling of miracles.

CONVERSATIONAL STYLE AND HIGH DRAMA

A final rhetorical appeal of Benny Hinn is his stage presence. Conversational style, good looks, and high drama help make up an interesting and pleasing presentation.

With his good sense of humor and conversational style, Benny Hinn is a likeable guy. In a word, he is charming. Once he asked his Nashville crowd how many came by bus and how many came alone. Then he asked, much to the delight of the audience, "how many were forced?" The crowd burst out in laughter. Hinn frequently jokes with his audiences, making them feel at ease. Writing for *Saturday Night* magazine, David Lees correctly describes Hinn as "charming, feckless, self-effacing, and . . . cute." Lees points out that Hinn's "naivety" and "self-mocking humour" have helped him capture followers (56).

Like his idol Kathryn Kuhlman Hinn is also ecumenical, embracing people of all faiths. This, too, leads to his attraction. He takes the position that "as long as Jesus is your savior, nothing can defeat you" whether one is Pentecostal, Baptist, Lutheran, or Catholic. In short, Hinn appears to be the type of person one would like to know on a personal level. He is friendly, personable, likeable, positive, and humble all in one.

In general, Benny Hinn's language is vivid. Speaking in a Middle Eastern accent, prior to the start of his Friday night sermon, Hinn warned his excited audience, "Ladies and Gentlemen, put your seatbelts on. We're about to take off." The audience roared with approval. Hinn's expressiveness can also be seen in one of his favorite quips: "If we only have the power, we'll blow up. If we only have the Word, we'll dry up. If we have both, we'll grow up." When coaxing people to give to Benny Hinn Media Ministries, he reassures his audience that "Everything you give goes into your account in glory." Such graphic language is lively and interesting and helps to endear Hinn to those watching.

Aside from his expressive language he is a showman on stage. His performances are theatrical. Hinn himself confesses that "there's a little bit of show business" in what he does ("Impact") and realizes how important histrionics are in maintaining a following. In an interview with *Charisma* magazine, he once disclosed, "There is pressure to produce when you're up there on that platform. People don't come just to hear you preach; they want to see something" (Davis D7).

If "seeing something" is what people want, then "producing" is what Hinn does. He walks freely around the platform when preaching or performing healings, holding a cordless microphone in one hand and occasionally raising both arms above his head as he stretches them out toward heaven, coat open and shirt sleeves protruding. Often he takes off his coat and rolls up his sleeves. He has also been known to throw his coat across the stage while running at people to slay them in the spirit.

Normally, when slaying people in the spirit, Hinn places a hand on their forehead, at which point they fall backward into an usher's arms and are then gently laid on the floor. Sometimes he merely waves his hand at them or rushes at them while waving his arms in the air. It is common for ushers standing behind individuals to fall under the power themselves. During this phase of his service, Hinn too, may come under the power and stagger backward where he is caught just in time by a nearby usher before knocking over a music stand or crashing into the drum set or grand piano beside him. Audiences roar with laughter whenever they see these on-stage antics. If entertainment is what people come to see, then they certainly do not go away disappointed. Between the sensational claims about the miraculous Hinn makes on stage and his physical capers, the fun factor at these crusades is off the scale.

In commenting on Hinn's on-stage theatrics, "televangelist watchdog" Ole Anthony said of Hinn, "He's just goofy" ("Impact"). Hinn's platform behavior has also brought him criticism even from charismatics like evangelist James Robison: "I told him [Hinn] God didn't anoint him to preach erroneous teachings and perform extravagant theatrics like knocking people down, waving his coat around, and blowing on people, and, if he continued, his ministry would be destroyed within three years" (Ferraiuolo 38). Apparently Robison was wrong because it has been more than three years since he warned Hinn, but Hinn continues to flourish. Sadly, it is partly because of these "erroneous teachings" and "extravagant theatrics" that Hinn maintains his popularity.

CONCLUSION

Like other healing evangelists in this book, Hinn has learned the secret to rhetorical success. He is humble and self-effacing, giving God the credit for the healings and taking none for himself. He employs scriptural references, leaving his Pentecostal and charismatic followers with the impression that what he teaches is grounded in the Word. He understands the value of testimony—both that of others and his own—in inducing people to believe in miracles. His personal stories of being healed or visited by Jesus or an angel go a long way in convincing his audiences. Hank Hanegraaff, an outspoken critic of Hinn, has made the observation "that Hinn has achieved popularity largely through his oral and written accounts of frequent, intense, and direct interaction with the supernatural" (Frame 54). These testimonies become even more powerful when backed by physical demonstrations and told within a setting of empty wheelchairs and discarded crutches, walkers, and oxygen tanks.

Hinn's willingness and ability to draw on the influence of Kathryn Kuhlman also add to his ethos. Finally, his good looks, conversational and charming style, humor, ecumenical approach, vivid language, and flamboyant stage presence make him a pleasing personality to watch. With all of this going for him, is there any wonder why Hinn is so convincing about the miraculous?

CNN reporter John Camp once made the observation that Benny Hinn "gives hope to the hopeless." This appears to be what Hinn wants to do—in part, at least. Hinn once said, "If Benny Hinn can give people one thing, I'm satisfied. And that's hope." Even though Hinn recognizes that not everyone at his crusades who claims to be healed actually receives a healing, he is willing to continue. To Benny, helping just one person is enough to justify his faith healing ministry. From the size of his following, it appears that Hinn is bringing hope not to just a few but to "hundreds of thousands of people" ("Impact"). Moreover, his popularity is not likely to be abated any time soon.

REFERENCES

Bearden, Michelle. "Benny Hinn." *Publishers Weekly* 10 Feb. 1992: 42+.

"Covenant Partners in Ministry." *Benny Hinn Media Ministries*. Online. Internet. Aug. 1997: http://www.bennyhinn.org/.

Davis, James D. "Benny Hinn." *The Phoenix Gazette* 11 Sept. 1993: D6–D7.

Ferraiuolo, Perucci. "Christian Leaders Admonish Hinn." *Christianity Today* 16 Aug. 1993: 38–39.

Frame, Randy. "Same Old Benny Hinn, Critics Say." *Christianity Today* 5 Oct. 1997: 52–54.

Gray, Carol. Letter to the author. 13 July 1998.

Hinn, Benny. *Good Morning, Holy Spirit*. Nashville: Thomas Nelson, 1990.

"Impact." Narr. John Camp. CNN. 23 November 1997.

Lees, David. "Blow Me Down Jesus." *Saturday Night* Dec. 94/Jan. 95: 50+.

Midday Newscast. CBS. WTVF, Nashville. 24 Oct. 1997.

"Ministry Profile." *Benny Hinn Media Ministries*. Online. Internet. Aug. 1997: http://www.bennyhinn.org/.

"Miracles from Singapore." *This is Your Day*. Trinity Broadcasting Network. 12 Nov. 1997.

CHAPTER EIGHT

Their Speech Betrayeth Them

If there is an implicit rhetorical theory (i.e., distinguishing rhetorical traits) of various groups of individuals as Otis Walter suggests, the question arises: What is the implicit rhetorical theory of twentieth-century American faith healers? What distinguishing marks do they possess? How was it, in other words, that they were so successful in selling the idea of miraculous healings to their audiences? Although there may be subtle differences in the personalities discussed in this book, those faith healers examined herein relied—consciously or unconsciously—on similar techniques to convince their audiences that miraculous healings are normative for the twentieth century.

RHETORICAL CHARACTERISTICS

Rhetorical Exigencies

First it should be noted that the rhetorical exigencies for faith healers across this century were the same. All provided hope to those who had all but given up hope. Twentieth-century faith healers merely responded to the maladies of the people of their day. Although the racial, religious, and economic demographics of audiences may have varied slightly from one healing evangelist to another, the fact is faith healers catered to those with physical infirmities. This much did not change from one personality to another. Indeed, this became part of the reason for their existence.

As has been suggested in previous chapters, whenever individuals exhaust all medical possibilities for improvement, often the only place to turn is toward someone preaching the possibility—even the probability—of a miraculous cure from God. This option is particularly appealing if a person believes in God in the first place. And, twentieth-century Americans have never been short on faith in God. A Gallup Poll conducted in 1944, for example, showed that ninety-six percent of all Americans "believe in a God" (*Gallup Poll* vol. 1, 473). In 1954 the figure was identical (*Gallup Poll* vol. 2, 1293). In 1968 the number rose to ninety-eight percent (*Gallup Poll* vol. 3, 2174). In 1976 ninety-four percent answered yes when asked if they believe in God (*Gallup Poll* vol. 2, 627).

Of course technically speaking, one can believe in God without believing in miracles, but a modicum of surveys have shown that many who believe in God also believe in the miraculous. For example, as recently as December 1997, according to the Pew Research Center, seventy-one percent reported that they believe in God. This poll also revealed that sixty-one percent believe in miracles (Aversa 3A). A Gallup Poll conducted in the early 1990s showed that as many as eight out of ten Americans believed in miracles (Long 1).

Although very few Gallup Polls per se across the twentieth century have directly asked Americans if they believe in miracles, a 1962 poll showed that one out of every five—or approximately twenty million Americans—reported having had a "moment of sudden religious insight or awakening." Gallup Poll reporters found that these experiences covered five areas: (1) a "mystic experience"; (2) the conviction that one's sins were forgiven and salvation was granted; (3) the belief that prayers were answered in a "miraculous" way; (4) the "reassurance" of God's love and power in a moment of crisis; and (5) "visions, dreams, or voices" (*Gallup Poll* vol. 3, 1762–63). Items three and five, and perhaps one and four, clearly fit into the category of the miraculous.

While Gallup Polls throughout the twentieth century generally have not questioned Americans' belief in the miraculous, survey after survey has shown that Americans have consistently believed in God. Further, many Americans who reportedly believe in God probably also believe in miracles. This much is obvious by the thousands upon thousands who flocked to the crusades of various faith healers across the twentieth century. Gilbert pointed out in 1988, "Nearly every American believes in God, a being they think of as creator, healer, friend, redeemer, and father" (303). This could be said about Americans throughout this century.

When many Americans who believe in God and the miraculous are physically afflicted beyond any help doctors might be able to provide, they become prime candidates to attend the healing services of individuals selling miraculous cures. These types of individuals, along with their loved ones who accompanied them, made up a significant portion of the audiences of twentieth-century faith healers. They had high hopes that something good would happen to them.

Given the fact that humans will always suffer from sickness and affliction there is no reason to believe that healing evangelists will likely disappear in the coming centuries. This becomes especially true as long as individuals believe in God and grant the possibility of the miraculous. In any event the personalities in the present study operated largely in response to the demands placed upon them by their physically ailing constituencies. They made successful careers out of trying to help those in desperate need.

To God Give the Glory

One thing that contributed to the popularity of the faith healers in this study, as well as to their selling of the miraculous, is the fact that none claimed to have personal power to heal people. All the credit was given to God.

Two things should be noted here. First these individuals *truly* believed that they themselves could not heal, that any power to heal came from God who worked through them. Moreover, no one would receive a healing without faith that God could make him or her whole. This later teaching is why healing revivalists have been labeled "faith healers" by the press and the general public in the first place. Second, and perhaps more important from a rhetorical standpoint, faith healers' claims that they had no power made them appear humble before their audiences, thus obviating any ill will that could have arisen should the speaker have taken credit for any good done. Faith healers throughout this century understood this and went to great lengths to remind their audiences to give God the credit lest their followers perceive them as arrogant and stop listening to their preaching.

We Came from Nothing

In addition to the claim that they had no personal power to perform miracles, twentieth-century faith healers in general, often reminded their followers of their own less-than-ideal beginnings. Whether it was Aimee Semple McPherson reminding her audiences of the fact that she was just a farm girl, William Branham, Oral Roberts, A. A. Allen, and Ernest Angley telling their followers of how poor they were while growing up, or Kathryn Kuhlman reminding her audiences of her ordinariness as an untalented, small-town girl from Concordia, Missouri they used such stories to their benefit. Even Benny Hinn, while not poor, per se, articulated personal hardships he endured as a boy and adolescent before going into the ministry.

These narratives about humble origins not only served to create identification with blue-collar audiences but reminded listeners that the evangelists themselves had not forgotten their roots. In short they had not become too proud to minister to the poor and feeble despite their success. Further, these stories served as inspiration to the down and out that with God all things are possible, that there is hope for a brighter future. If God could raise up someone ordinary like Kathryn Kuhlman, for instance, surely He could spare a little mercy to heal someone with diabetes or arthritis.

If He Can Heal Me, He Can Heal Anyone

One of the most effective rhetorical techniques for convincing listeners that anyone can receive a miraculous healing is the personal testimony of someone who claims to have experienced such a miracle. In this way an individual perpetuates the notion of miraculous cures. Thus, when one person hears another testify about his or her healing, that individual soon believes that he or she, too, can receive a healing and the process continues.

Not only did twentieth-century faith healers, in general, rely on their own personal example to convince their audiences of healing, but they also testified about miracles that they themselves supposedly had witnessed. They also relied on the testimony of someone who claimed to have been healed, sometimes even bringing them back to another service months after their "healing" to testify on behalf of God and His evangelist.

It is difficult for an audience who already believes in God not to believe in the miraculous when they are constantly bombarded with such positive testimonies. These audiences lacked the knowledge and the critical thinking skills not to become swept away either by the evangelist or by other people who came to the stage to offer their stories of how they were healed of some life-threatening ailment. Like audiences sold on any consumer product after hearing someone testify about how wonderful the product has made their life, so too, were audiences sold on miraculous cures after listening to people testify about their "cures."

It is safe to say that as long as faith healing is a part of the American culture, testimony will probably always play an integral role in such services—just as it does in the advertisement of any product or service. Faith healing evangelists clearly understand the rhetorical power inherent in one individual standing under the spotlight in a moment of glory before a large audience and explaining how God had miraculously brought him or her back from physical destruction. Further, whenever personal testimony is coupled with a physical demonstration of, say, someone bending over and touching his or her toes to demonstrate a lack of back pain, or climbing out of a wheelchair, it becomes even more difficult not to believe. Audiences simply are either not willing or do not know enough to ask the critical question of just how sick a person might have been before he or she came into the auditorium. They are not privy to that type of information. All audiences see is someone running around on stage or rising from a wheelchair, even though in all likelihood, these people could have walked into the auditorium on their own in the first place.

What is intriguing to this author is how audiences raved and swooned over people walking around on stage claiming a miracle, when often they walked with a bad limp, clearly indicating that no organic change had occurred. Perhaps philosopher David Hume explains it best when he suggests, "If the spirit of religion join itself to the love of wonder, there is an end of common sense. . . . A religionist may be an enthusiast, and imagine he sees what has no reality . . ." (Swinburne 15).

If the Bible Says So, It Must Be So

One thing that all faith healers in this study had in common was their constant reference to passages in the Bible as proof for the miraculous. This became an effective rhetorical device because their constituencies already believed the Bible to be the inspired word of God, and everything it said—they believed—was directly relevant to their lives. Thus, twentieth-century faith healers perpetuated a belief system that their audiences already accepted.

As long as a passage from the Bible appeared even remotely related to healing, faith healers successfully employed it to prove to their listeners that they could be miraculously cured. And what is perhaps even more puzzling is the fact that some passages which said nothing about healing were occasionally invoked. Hebrews 13:8 ("Jesus Christ is the same yesterday and today, yea and for ever"), for example, was probably quoted as often as any verse to prove the miraculous, yet is says nothing about healing at all. The fact that Jesus is the same yesterday, today, and forever does not necessarily mean that He performs miracles today like those recorded in the New Testament. Hebrews 13:8 is simply referring to the essence of Jesus' character not his method of operation (i.e., performance of miracles.) Strictly speaking, if Jesus were the same yesterday, today, and forever, in the sense that faith healers interpret this passage, then He should be alive today performing miracles exactly as is recorded in the synoptic gospels. The fact is, Jesus is not on earth today performing any miracle nor are any of his disciples or human representatives.

If Hebrews 13:8 does not teach the miraculous then why have faith healers used this passage so successfully throughout the twentieth century? The answer lies in the fact that audiences simply have not critically examined its meaning. Like other passages, they have heard it for so long that they have blindly come to accept it as teaching what the faith healer says it teaches. Hebrews 13:8 has become part of the healing culture, part of what one expects to hear whenever he or she attends a healing revival. Hebrews 13:8, along with other oft-quoted passages, is consonant with the whole healing scene. It is what one expects to hear.

Another favorite passage used by twentieth-century faith healers is Isaiah 53:5, also found in part in I Peter 2:24—the idea that "with his stripes we are healed." Twentieth-century faith healers taught that Christ's death on the cross not only assured spiritual atonement but vouchsafed physical healing as well. The problem is, like with so many other verses, faith healers, and those who follow them, have taken this passage out of its context.

Here Isaiah, in referring to Christ's death on the cross, points out that He was "wounded for our transgressions" and "bruised for our iniquities," things of a spiritual nature. Isaiah follows these thoughts with the idea of being healed by Christ's stripes. He then closes the paragraph by revealing that since "we like sheep have gone astray," God laid on Christ "the iniquity of us all." The principles that both precede and follow the phrase "by whose stripes ye are healed" are spiritual in nature, thus making this phrase spiritual as well.

Hank Hanegraaff, one of the most outspoken critics of faith teachers today, argues that "it is common knowledge that the Hebrew word *raphah* [translated "healed" in the above verse] often refers to spiritual rather than physical healing." Hanegraaff continues, "Isaiah could hardly make it more clear that he has spiritual healing in mind when he writes that the Messiah (Christ) was to be pierced for our transgressions and crushed for our iniquities (Isaiah 53:5)" (250).

The same spiritual notions can be found in I Peter 2:24–25. Here Peter discusses the fact that Christ "bare our sins . . . upon the tree, that we, having died unto sins, might live unto righteousness; by whose stripes ye were healed." Peter, using the same pastoral metaphor that Isaiah used, suggests that "ye were going astray like sheep; but are now returned unto the Shepherd and Bishop of your souls [Christ]." How much clearer could Peter have made the point that Christ's death on the cross provided a spiritual, not a physical, benefit? It is difficult to understand how those who use this verse to prove physical healing cannot see its spiritual context.

Hanegraaff argues that if Isaiah 53:5 and I Peter 2:24–25 referred to physical healing, as well as spiritual healing, that presents a problem for faith healers. "If healing is in the atonement and is accessed by faith, then those who die due to lack of faith must remain in their sins. They die without hope. Why? Because if both healing and salvation are included in this passage, they must be accessed in the same way. And if one does not have enough faith to make oneself well, it follows that he cannot have enough faith to be saved" (250). What faith healer would be willing to agree with this conclusion?

Suffice it to say that as long as a passage from the Bible even remotely appeared to be related to healing, faith healers seized it as proof text for their practice in spite of the fact that the verse was taken out of its context or interpreted to mean something it does not mean. It was difficult for audiences to deny the assertions of faith healers based on some reference to the scriptures because they already believed the Bible was their guide. They would not, therefore, dare contradict the evangelist when he or she identified some scripture that seemed to imply healing, however remote the passage might have been and despite the fact that they truly had not witnessed anything sensational.

DYNAMIC PERSONALITIES

In addition to the above factors, the rhetorical appeal of twentieth-century faith healers featured their dynamic personalities and stage presence. This, coupled with their physical beauty or handsomeness, in most cases, was one of their greatest attractions. Lewis argues that the "superior ability to communicate verbally and nonverbally may result in the attribution of charisma to a leader/communicator," thereby causing an audience to be attracted to him or her. Factors such as "vocal force," "rapid delivery," and "nonverbal qualities" all contribute to make "charismatic figures" popular (106). These characteristics certainly worked for the faith healers in this study.

Aimee Semple McPherson put on one of the best shows in town (Austin 3). In addition to her illustrated sermons this physically attractive female was about as animated on stage as a person could be. Despite his short stature and simplistic approach, William Branham commanded peoples' attention with his boldness and conversational style. Oral Roberts preached loud and hard, hair all the while drooping on his forehead. A. A. Allen jumped around in the pulpit like an acrobat. Perhaps not since the days of Billy Sunday have American religious audiences seen a more energetic preacher than A. A. Allen. Ernest Angley's dynamism showed in his strong and idiosyncratic vocal inflections which borderlined on the bizarre. Kathryn Kuhlman's drama played out in her voice and physical appearance. Benny Hinn's running around on stage, ripping off his coat, and yelling into the microphone make him—along with A. A. Allen—one of the most dramatic figures of the entire twentieth-century. If they were nothing else, twentieth-century American faith healers were fun to listen to and to watch. In a word, they were entertaining. There can be no doubt that their showmanship served to attract and persuade large audiences at a time.

WILL THE REAL MIRACLE PLEASE STAND UP?

Understanding the types of "miracles" that occurred in the services of twentieth-century healing evangelists raises the question about the validity of their claims. To borrow the words of McCarron regarding the "miracles" of contemporary televangelists, there was "nothing astonishing" about the "healings" of twentieth-century faith healers. Or, as McCarron puts it, they were utterly "mundane" (29). So, no matter how much an individual might have claimed a miraculous healing in his or her heart, this did not make one healed. What is ironic is that the miracles one reads about in the Bible were different in several significant ways from the so-called miracles that occurred in the services of faith healers in the twentieth century. This is problematic because twentieth-century faith healers used the scriptures so frequently and adamantly as proof of the miraculous, yet by the standard of judgment they set for themselves, they failed miserably.

Before going further a critical observation should be made. There are many individuals who do not believe the accounts of the miraculous as listed in the Bible in the first place (see Kurtz, for example). My purpose here is not to argue this issue one way or another. For our purposes it matters little whether one believes the Biblical accounts of such occurrences. What is important is that all of the faith healers we have examined in this book did and used them as a basis to believe in miracles in the twentieth century. However, a close look reveals that these evangelists' "miracles" were in no way comparable, even though they insisted, based on their interpretation of Hebrews 13:8, that Jesus operated in their day just as described in the New Testament. Or to borrow the words of Gloria Copeland, a contemporary faith healer, "nothing is changed" (Copeland, Oct. 17, 1992). To reiterate the point, twentieth-century faith healers failed miserably when judged by the standard that they set for themselves—the Bible. Here is how.

First, Biblical miracles always involved a violation of the laws of nature, which incidentally, is how both philosopher David Hume and theologian C. S. Lewis define them (see Swinburne 14, 70). In Genesis 17, for example, is recorded the conception of Isaac to Sarah at the age of ninety. The laws of nature suggest that a woman, left on her own, cannot conceive at that age. Yet the Bible records how Sarah conceived and eventually gave birth. While the conception could be considered miraculous, since laws of nature tell us it is impossible for a woman to conceive at the age of ninety, the birth, per se, was not.

A similar argument could be made about the virgin birth of Christ as recorded in the New Testament. Christian theologian C. S. Lewis argues, "If God creates a miraculous spermatozoon in the body of a virgin, it does not proceed to break any laws. The laws at once take it over. Nature is ready. Pregnancy follows, according to all the normal laws, and nine months later a child is born" (Lewis 59).

Many who believe in twentieth-century miracles—as do many friends of this author—fallaciously point out that the birth of a baby is a miracle. Kathryn Kuhlman, herself, believed this (Kuhlman 20). The fact is births of any species are no more miraculous than thunderstorms. They happen in nature all of the time. Women have been giving birth for thousands of years. How can something that occurs naturally be called miraculous? C. S. Lewis argues that in order for some event to be labeled a miracle it must "interrupt the orderly march of events, the steady development of nature according to her own interest, genius or character" (Swinburne 70). Conception in virgins and ninety-year-old women would clearly "interrupt the orderly march of events" and could be classified as miraculous, but births themselves in no way violate nature. Therefore, they cannot be considered miracles.

In Exodus 4, when God called Moses to lead the Israelites out of Egyptian captivity, Moses was reluctant to obey for fear that the Israelites would not believe that God had called him. The Bible reveals how God empowered Moses with three "signs" in an attempt to demonstrate Moses' calling to the elders of the Israelites. First, Moses changed a rod into a serpent and then back into a rod. Second, he placed his hand inside his coat and pulled it out, revealing a leprous hand. Then he placed the same hand back into his coat and withdrew it, revealing a healthy, healed hand all of which occurred spontaneously. Finally, he poured water from the river onto the land and it turned into blood. When Moses performed these "signs" to the Israelites, the Bible records that they "believed" and "worshipped." Why did they believe? They believed because these events did not occur in nature and that anyone performing them must have been sent by God, a supernatural force. In fact, this was the very argument that Nicodemus made to Jesus in the New Testament in John 3:2: "Rabbi, we know that thou art a teacher come from God; for no one can do these signs that thou doest, except God be with him."

In I Kings 18, in the contest on Mount Carmel with the prophets of Baal, Elijah instantaneously called fire down out of heaven to consume an altar that had been dowsed with water. When the people saw the sopping altar immediately consumed by fire from heaven, the Bible records that the people "fell on their faces" and believed in God. As in the case of Moses, the miracle performed by Elijah produced faith in the audience because of its violation of the laws of nature.

In the New Testament one can read of Jesus walking on water (Matthew 14:25), turning water into wine (John 2), or restoring Malchus' ear to the side of his head (John 18:2–12; Luke 22:51), among others. All of these instances involved a contradiction of the laws of nature. Faith healers in the twentieth century have never conducted a feat similar to those above. Furthermore, it is doubtful whether they even understood the basic premise behind a miracle (i.e., a violation of the laws of nature).

A second characteristic of Biblical miracles is that they were always immediate. That is, there was no waiting period for the person to be healed. Whether it involved a man being healed of leprosy (Matthew 8), blind men receiving their sight (Matthew 9), or a palsied man being able to walk (Mark 2) all healings occurred instantaneously. "Straightway" and "immediately" are terms the scriptures employ over and over again to describe many healings in the New Testament (Matthew 8:3; Mark 2:12; Luke 4:39; and Acts 3:7). Contrast these healings to those of twentieth-century faith healers who often told people that it would take a few days for a person to improve. Or as Ernest Angley once told an individual after he ostensibly received a miracle, "Go and get well" (Observation by the author, Feb. 19, 1988). Warner makes the observation that in the revivals of Kathryn Kuhlman, Oral Roberts, Jack Coe, and William Branham there were "very few verifiable cases of instantaneous healings" (145). I have personally attended the healing revivals of Ernest Angley, Benny Hinn, and Gloria Copeland. Moreover, I have watched dozens of television programs and videorecordings of William Branham, Oral Roberts, A. A. Allen, Ernest Angley, Kathryn Kuhlman, and Benny Hinn but have yet to see anything remotely resembling an instantaneous cure.

A third characteristic of Biblical miracles is that they were always complete. The man with a withered hand in Matthew 12:13, for example, was "restored whole." The lame man healed in Acts 4:9 was made "whole." There was never any hint of recurring side effects. William Nolen records how some in Kathryn Kuhlman's audiences had to go back to their medicines or medical apparatuses after their so-called healings. Others died shortly after their healings, thinking they were healed when in reality they were not (see Nolen 37–91).

A fourth characteristic of Biblical miracles is that they could be verified with one's own eyes. Simply put, individuals could know on the spot if any miracle had occurred or not because they could see an organic change. It is difficult for a contemporary audience to say that a miracle has not occurred when it is impossible to see any change in the first place. In this way they are non-falsifiable.

In Luke 7:11–17 the Widow's son of Nain was pronounced dead. Luke records that Jesus raised him. In John 9 Jesus healed a blind man whom everyone had known to be blind from birth. Placing Malchus' ear back on the side of his head (John 18:2–12) could be seen by everyone and verified on the spot by anyone looking. A close look reveals that the types of miracles that twentieth-century faith healers performed were unlike any of these. Instead they were non-empirical and hence, non-provable. For instance, one cannot see weak eyes, back problems, poor blood circulation, arthritis, diabetes, and addiction to alcohol, cigarettes, and drugs being healed, yet these were consistently the types of ailments that were supposedly cured during the religious services of twentieth-century faith healers. Ironically, these miracles in no way compared to the types of empirical miracles that one reads about in the Bible. One cannot judge on the spot whether arthritis, diabetes, poor blood circulation, and so forth were healed. In this way they were non-falsifiable. Moreover, those looking on really did not know to what extent someone was afflicted with these ailments in the first place since they could not be seen with the eyes. Audiences have to take people at their word when they testify to what extent they were sick but now healed. On their face there is nothing amazing in these types of demonstrations.

A fifth characteristic of Biblical healings is that they caused astonishment on the part of the people who witnessed them. The New Testament suggests that when individuals were healed crowds were "all amazed and glorified God" (Mark 2:12); "were amazed . . . with a great amazement" (Mark 5:42); or "were filled with wonder and amazement" (Acts 3:8–10). Even Jesus' enemies were amazed at his healings (Matthew 12:22–ff). Seeing that they could not deny the miracle itself, the best that they could do was to attribute Jesus' power to Satan. In Acts 4 even skeptics did not dare deny Peter and John's healing of the lame man. They confessed that "a notable miracle" had been performed, that everyone in Jerusalem knew it, and that they could not deny it. The interesting thing about the above examples is that when miracles were recorded in the New Testament, people were astonished. Even the most hardened critics did not deny them. Moreover, no emotionally charged atmosphere like one would witness in most of the healing services of twentieth-century healers was necessary to cause astonishment or belief in a so-called miraculous healing. If anything "miracles" of twentieth-century faith healers caused skepticism, not astonishment.

A sixth characteristic of Biblical healings is that they were unlimited in scope. In other words it did not matter what the ailment or affliction was. People were healed of it. Biblical healings ranged from body parts being placed back onto people, to totally blind people receiving their sight, to lame people walking, to skin diseases being spontaneously healed, to dead people being raised.

When this writer visited Grace Cathedral in February 1988, he sat behind a gentleman who looked to be a regular patron of Angley's Friday night miracle service by the way he responded to Angley's cues. This gentleman had a permanently closed right eye. If God were performing miracles through Angley like he claims He does, then why could Angley not open this individual's eye? Why is it that withered body parts were not made whole during the services of faith healers? Why is it that missing body parts were never regenerated? And why is it that healing revivalists never raised dead people, A. A. Allen's and others' claims to have done so notwithstanding? In fact one woman reportedly died during Ernest Angley's 1978 New Year's Day healing service (Sims 149). The fact is that miracles like one reads about in the Bible did not occur in the healing services of twentieth-century faith healers.

A final characteristic of New Testament healings is that, ironically, they generally occurred without faith on the part of the recipient. And this flies right in the face of faith healers' claims. Sometimes those healed knew nothing about the healer at all (John 5:13). Sometimes those healed were not even alive to have faith in the first place. Sometimes if a healing failed to occur it was due to the faithlessness of the healer, not the person being healed (Matt. 17:14–21). Faith healers, and those who believe in them, simply do not realize this about healings that are recorded in the New Testament. No faith healer in the twentieth century would take responsibility for a failed healing. The responsibility was always placed on the person seeking the healing.

In general Biblical miracles were performed to produce faith (not skepticism) in the hearts of audiences. They were invoked to demonstrate that the person performing the miracles had been sent from God, not for social purposes and certainly not to raise money for some charismatic spokesperson to continue his or her ministry. Both the examples of Moses and Elijah cited above, demonstrate this point. It was not until they performed their signs to their audiences that their audiences believed they had the mantle of God upon them.

The New Testament depicts Jesus as performing miracles to convince his audiences that he had been sent by God. In John 3 John records how Nicodemus told Jesus that he believed Jesus had been sent by God because no man could do the miraculous that Jesus had done unless God was with him. In Matthew 9 Jesus, in a move to prove that he had the right to forgive sins (i.e., that he was God in the flesh) commanded a palsied man to stand up and walk. Jesus understood that anyone could claim to forgive sins, but not just anyone could back up the claim with an empirically-verifiable healing which is why he told the man to take up his bed and walk.

The New Testament records that even Jesus' apostles performed miracles to demonstrate that they had been commissioned by God (see Acts 5:12–14; II Cor. 12:12; and Hebrews 2:3–4, for example). Faith healers of the twentieth century and those who believe in them have things backward. They believe that one has to have faith before the miraculous can occur. Throughout the Bible, however, miracles caused faith rather than faith causing the miraculous as twentieth-century faith healers would have audiences believe.

What faith healers claim to have done throughout the twentieth century are not true miracles. Rather, they might better be described by McCarron as "contingency" miracles. According to him "contingency" miracles are miracles "only because the believer interprets them that way." They serve as "legitimating apparatuses in that they show the theist what particular issues are presently of such importance that God would apply his divine hand to direct events to a specific end." "Though contingency miracles may appear mundane and lifeless at first look," claims McCarron, "they become vital forces for socio-political legitimation. . . ." In other words, they serve as a justification for the belief of a "socially constructed world." The value of contingency miracles, therefore, is not in their ability to astonish those who view them but in their efficacy to solidify people "while further insulating [a] worldview from the larger sphere of secular life" (20, 29–30). There can be no doubt that such-type "miracles" solidified audiences throughout the twentieth century but also operated to attract large followings for the faith healers of this study.

In spite of this, what are we to make of individuals who swear to have received a miraculous cure at the hands of a twentieth-century faith healer? Certainly, they are not in short supply and can be found in almost any city or town in America, often boldly—and occasionally even confrontationally—challenging the skeptic to explain how it was that they were healed. Nickell points out that healing naturally occurs in the body. Wounds, broken bones, and infections often respond to the body's self-healing processes by themselves. In fact, according to Nickell, one estimation suggests that seventy-five percent of all patients would improve if they received no medical help at all. Even certain types of cancers often undergo "spontaneous remission." Multiple sclerosis and other diseases can "abate" for as little as a few months or as long as several years. Nickell contends, "Although the nature of such remissions is still not fully understood by medical science, the fact of their unpredictable occurrence is well documented. If a remission or regression occurs any time after a faith healer has performed his ritualistic ministrations, it may be falsely attributed to the healer's intervention" (133–34).

It might also be that an individual coming into a faith healer's assembly believes he or she has a certain type of illness when in reality that illness has been misdiagnosed. Nickell cites the example of a young woman who claimed to have had an inoperable tumor on her brain stem, which supposedly had been confirmed by a CT scan. The dark spots on the scan, however, upon further investigation, turned out to be little more than imperfections in the scanning process. The woman had not really had a tumor to begin with.

Additionally any number of illnesses are "highly responsive to the power of suggestion." They are known as psychosomatic illnesses and range "from back pains to hysterical blindness." The requirement for a psychosomatic cure, says Nickell, is merely a patient's belief in what a practitioner promises. Nickell goes on to point out, "Just as physical ailments can be exacerbated by worry and other forms of stress, positive attitudes seem to enhance the body's healing capacities" (134). Harvard professor and medical doctor Herbert Benson agrees that "there are cases where faith healers bring about cures." "Many people do get better," suggests Dr. Benson, "but it may not be the faith healer that's doing it. It may be their belief in the faith healer and what the faith healer represents" ("Impact"; see Benson).

Pain is also susceptible to the power of suggestion which may account for why so many people, upon bending over and touching their toes as proof of their healing, testify to having no pain. Such absence of pain is due to the body's release of endorphins. Absence of pain, however, does not necessarily mean that a person is healed. Nickell cogently argues, "In the excitement of an evangelical revival, the reduction of pain due to endorphin release often causes people to believe and act as if they have been miraculously healed, whereas later investigation reveals their situation is as bad—or even worse—than before. It is the illusion, however, and not the reality that is witnessed by thousands and cited as 'proof' of miraculous cures" (135–36).

CONCLUSION

In this book I have attempted to demonstrate a rhetorical genre of twentieth-century American faith healers by looking at the most prominent men and women who engaged in the practice. My intent was to address the question of how faith healers sold the idea of miraculous cures to their audiences.

While each faith healer may have run his or her church or organization differently from the others, and while each individual may have conducted his or her revivals and healing services slightly different than the others, all relied on very similar strategies in attempting to persuade their followers. And what's more, with a few exceptions here and there, the audiences for all faith healers, starting with Aimee Semple McPherson and ending with Benny Hinn, were alike in at least one critical way. They all contained the sick and afflicted who were looking to be cured. Many audience members had all but abandoned hope after realizing that medical science could provide no remedy.

It is not likely that one will ever find a case of a faith healer in this century ever taking credit for any miracle he or she believes occurred. This runs against the Christian concept of humility and self-deprecation. Furthermore, it would be rhetorical suicide and faith healers understand this all too well.

Not only do faith healers never take the credit, but they often relay how God chose them, among all people with no special advantage in life, to perform His work. When audiences hear the rags-to-riches stories that faith healers tell, this serves to persuade them of the miraculous. After all how could faith healers be so successful, so well off after being so poor, unless God had anointed them?

Testimonies play an integral role in the persuasive process of twentieth-century faith healers. Whether it is the faith healer himself or herself relaying a personal cure from stuttering, tuberculosis, or the like, or whether it is someone standing before a mass audience swearing that they personally received a miraculous healing from God, it becomes difficult for an individual—especially a religious one—not to believe that he or she can be miraculously cured. After all, God is no respecter of persons.

Central to the persuasion process is the Bible. Had there been no Bible, there would be no twentieth-century faith healer. They take their license to practice from the scriptures, and they use them to convince others to believe as well. Hebrews 13:8 and Isaiah 53:5, among others, are commonly misapplied in support of the miraculous. These passages usually emerge in some of the most desultory sermons imaginable. Faith healers have had little, if any, formal training in the art of public speaking, and, therefore, pay little attention to organization of sermons. Audiences do not seem to mind, however.

Finally, faith healers have been some of the most interesting public speakers to watch. Their dynamic and sometimes strange on-stage antics make for an entertaining show. Whether waving their hands frantically in the air, jumping around on stage, or dramatically employing vocal inflection to emphasize a point, it is difficult not to take one's eyes and ears off of a twentieth-century faith healer, especially when such behavior is reinforced by some sensational claim.

And so, even though faith healers operated in various decades of the twentieth century, their rhetorical methods were essentially the same. Perhaps they learned these methods by watching each other. Certainly they must have learned by watching those of their previous generation. But, however they learned them, there can be no mistaking who they are and what twentieth-century religious figures are up to when one sees them tightly grip some crying subject's head in both hands and one hears the indelible phrase roll from their lips—"Foul Demons, Come Out!"

REFERENCES

Austin, Alvyn. *Aimee Semple McPherson*. Dan Mills, Ontario: Fitzhenry and Whiteside Limited, 1980.

Aversa, Jeannine. "Survey Finds Americans Increasingly Believe in God." *Wilmington Morning Star* 22 Dec. 1997: 3A

Benson, Herbert. *Timeless Healing: The Power and Biology of Belief*. New York: Scribner, 1996.

Copeland, Gloria. Sermon. Nashville, TN. 17 Oct. 1992.

The Gallup Poll: Public Opinion 1935–1948. Vol. 1. New York: Random House, 1972.

The Gallup Poll: Public Opinion 1972–1977. Vol. 2. Wilmington, DE: Scholarly Resources, Inc., 1978.

The Gallup Poll: Public Opinion 1935–1971. Vol. 3. New York: Random House, 1972.

Gilbert, Dennis A. *Compendium of American Public Opinion*. New York: Facts on File Publications, 1988.

Hanegraaff, Hank. *Christianity in Crisis*. Eugene, OR: Harvest House, 1993.

"Impact." Narr. John Camp. CNN. 23 November 1997.

Kuhlman, Kathryn. *I Believe in Miracles*. 1962. Old Tappan, NJ: Fleming H. Revell, 1970.

Kurtz, Paul. "The Biblical Roots of Faith Healing." *Free Inquiry* 14.1 (Winter 1993): 12. Online. Infotrac Search. University of North Carolina-Wilmington Lib. Internet. Feb. 1998.

Lewis, C. S. *Miracles*. New York: Macmillan Publishing Co., 1947.

Lewis, Todd V. "Charisma and Media Evangelists: An Explication and Model of Communication Influence." *The Southern Communication Journal* 54 (Fall 1988): 93–111.

Long, Karen Haymon. "Do Miracles Happen?" *The Tampa Tribune* 20 June 1993, metro ed., nation/world sec.: 1. Online. NewsFile Collection. University of North Carolina-Wilmington Lib. Internet. Feb. 1998.

McCarron, Gary. "Lost Dogs and Financial Healing: Deconstructing Televangelist Miracles." *The God Pumpers*. Eds. Marshall Fishwick and Ray B. Browne. Bowling Green, OH: Bowling Green State University Popular Press, 1987: 19–31.

Nickell, Joe. *Looking for a Miracle*. Buffalo, NY: Prometheus, 1993.

Nolen, William A. *Healing: A Doctor in Search of a Miracle*. New York: Random House, 1974.

Sims, Patsy. *Can Somebody Shout Amen!* New York: St. Martin's Press, 1988.

Swinburne, Richard. *The Concept of Miracle*. New York: Macmillan Publishing Co., 1970.

Walter, Otis M. "On the Varieties of Rhetorical Criticism." *Essays on Rhe-*

torical Criticism. Ed. Thomas R. Nilsen. New York: Random House, 1968. 158–72.

Warner, Wayne E. *The Woman Behind the Miracles*. Ann Arbor, MI: Servant Publications, 1993.

Index

About the Author

STEPHEN J. PULLUM is Associate Professor of Communication Studies and Associate Dean of the College of Arts and Sciences at the University of North Carolina at Wilmington. He has published numerous articles on religious rhetoric, and he is a former associate editor of the *Journal of Communication and Religion*.

ISBN 0-275-96083-8

90000>

EAN

9 780275 960834

HARDCOVER BAR CODE